THE NIGHT HERON

by **Jez Butterworth**

Cast in order of appearance
Wattmore **Karl Johnson**
Griffin **Ray Winstone**
Bolla **Jessica Stevenson**
Neddy **Roger Morlidge**
Royce **Paul Ritter**
Jonathan **Finlay Robertson**
Dougal **Geoffrey Church**

Director **Ian Rickson**
Designer **Ultz**
Lighting Designer **Mick Hughes**
Sound Designer **Paul Arditti**
Composer **Stephen Warbeck**
Assistant Director **Joseph Hill-Gibbins**
Assistant Designer **Robin Husband**
Casting Director **Lisa Makin**
Production Manager **Paul Handley**
Company Stage Manager **Cath Binks**
Stage Manager **Sara Chapman**
Deputy Stage Manager **Rachael Claire Lovett**
Assistant Stage Manager **Dani Youngman**
Costume Supervisor **Iona Kenrick**
Dialect Coach **Joan Washington**
Company Voice Work **Patsy Rodenburg**
Barn built by **Rupert Blakeley**

Royal Court Theatre would like to thank the following for their help with this production:
Amy Buscombe and BBC New Writing, Father Nick Mercer of St Mary's Presbytery SW1W, Dr Cleo Van Velsen, Suffolk Secrets, Stephen Jeffreys, the Tutor, Gardeners and Housekeeping staff of Pembroke College, Cambridge, Lec Refridgeration plc, McCain Foods (GB Ltd), Binoculars by Monk Optics Ltd - (01291689 858), Prop Portfolio Ltd, Propaganda, TDK UK Ltd. Wardrobe care by Persil and Comfort courtesy of Lever Fabergé.

THE COMPANY

Jez Butterworth (writer)
The Night Heron is Jez Butterworth's second play. His first, Mojo (1995), won the George Devine Award, the Olivier Award for Best Comedy and the Writer's Guild, Critics' Circle and Evening Standard Awards for Most Promising Playwright. In 1996 he directed a film adaptation of Mojo starring Ian Hart and Harold Pinter. This June sees the release of his second feature, Birthday Girl starring Nicole Kidman and Ben Chaplin.

Paul Arditti (sound designer)
Paul Arditti has been designing sound for theatre since 1983.
Royal Court productions include: Plasticine, Boy Gets Girl, Nightingale and Chase, Clubland, Blasted, Mouth To Mouth, Spinning Into Butter, I Just Stopped By To See The Man, Far Away, My Zinc Bed, 4.48 Psychosis, Fireface, Mr Kolpert, The Force of Change, Hard Fruit, Other People, Dublin Carol, The Glory of Living, The Kitchen, Rat in the Skull, Some Voices, Mojo, The Weir; Sliding With Suzanne, The Steward of Christendom, Shopping and Fucking, Blue Heart (co-productions with Out of Joint); The Chairs (co-production with Theatre de Complicite); Cleansed, Via Dolorosa.
Other theatre includes: Hinterland (Out of Joint); Afore Night Come (Young Vic); Tales From Hollywood (Donmar); Light (Complicite); Our Lady of Sligo (RNT with Out of Joint); Some Explicit Polaroids (Out of Joint); Hamlet, The Tempest (RSC); Orpheus Descending, Cyrano de Bergerac, St Joan (West End); Marathon (Gate).
Musicals include: Doctor Dolittle, Piaf, The Threepenny Opera.
Awards include: Drama Desk Award for Outstanding Sound Design 1992 for Four Baboons Adoring the Sun (Broadway).

Geoffrey Church
Theatre includes: The Day I Stood Still, The Beaux Stratagem (RNT); Return of the Prodigal, Artifice, Penny For a Song, His Majesty, The Dutch Courtesan (Orange Tree); A Jovial Crew (RNT Studio); Births, Marriages and Deaths (Nuffield, Southampton); She Stoops To Conquer (Sheffield); King Lear (Acter USA tour); The Rover (RSC); Much Ado About Nothing (Cheltenham); Richard II (Ludlow Festival); Sgt Musgrave's Dance, Plenty (Library, Manchester); Crimes of the Heart (Haymarket, Leicester).
Television includes: No Child of Mine (Best Single Drama, BAFTA winner), Lloyd and Hill, Holby City, Eastenders, Mind Games, Prime Suspect III, Capital City, Knuckle, Boon, Inspector Morse, Between the Lines, Wycliffe, Soldier, Soldier.

Joseph Hill-Gibbins (assistant director)
For the Royal Court as assistant director: Boy Gets Girl, Redundant, Blasted, Spinning Into Butter.
As assistant director, theatre includes: Hobson's Choice (Stephen Joseph Theatre, Scarborough); Corpse (Haymarket, Basingstoke); Woyzeck (Didsbury Studio, Manchester).
As director, theatre includes: Lonesome West (Manchester University); The Dark (also co-wrote), Rat In The Skull (Edinburgh Fringe).
Joseph is also a senior script reader at the Royal Court and a member of the Young Writers' Programme.
Joseph's work on this production is supported by the Channel Four/Royal Court Theatre Drama Directors Programme.

Mick Hughes (lighting designer)
For the Royal Court: The Shallow End, Ashes To Ashes.
Other theatre includes: Angels in America, Sweeney Todd, Dealer's Choice, House and Garden, No Man's Land (RNT); Wildest Dreams (RSC); Things We Do For Love, Peggy For You, Port Authority, The Homecoming (West End); Lizzie Finn, Give Me the Answer Do (Abbey, Dublin); Juno and the Paycock (Gaiety, Dublin); The Pinter Festival, Dublin Carol, Afterplay (Gate); Molly Sweeney (New York); Mahagonny (ENO); Damsels in Distress (currently on a national tour); The Pinter Festival at the Lincoln Centre, New York.
Mick has also worked in Vienna, Hong Kong, Toronto, Barcelona, Chicago, Pittsburgh and Washington since he started lighting plays in 1963.

Karl Johnson
For the Royal Court: Boy Gets Girl, The Weir, Been So Long, Just a Little Less than Normal, Sudlow's Dawn, Irish Eyes and English Tears.
Other theatre includes: The Walls, Cardiff East, The Ends of the Earth, The Machine Wreckers, Black Snow, The Resistible Rise of Arturo Ui, The Sea, Uncle Vanya, A Midsummer Night's Dream, Glengarry Glen Ross, Wild Honey, The Mysteries, Tim Page's Nam, Don Quixote, The Shape of the Table, The Rivals (RNT); In the Company of Men, TV Times, Knight of the Burning Pestle (RSC); Amadeus (Peter Hall Company); Woyzeck (Lyric, Hammersmith); War Crimes (ICA); The Dresser (Thorndike, Leatherhead); Hedda Gabler (Yvonne Arnauld, Guildford); As You Like It (Old Vic), Vieux Carre (Piccadilly).
Television includes: The Mayor of Casterbridge, Without Motive, David Copperfield, Vanity Fair, The Temptation of

Franz Schubert, Wing and a Prayer, An
Independent Man, As You Like It, Catherine The
Great, Lifeboat, Glassing Gareth, Judas and The
Gimp, Sexual Intercourse Began in 1963, The
Shawl, A Tale of Two Cities, Rules of
Engagement, Poirot, Casualty, The Bill, Boon,
Bergerac, Sons and Lovers, Rock Follies of 77,
Chips With Everything.
Films include: Love is the Devil, Wittgenstein,
Close My Eyes, Prick Up Your Ears, Jubilee, The
Tempest, The Tent, The Magic Shop, Soup, Pure.

Roger Morlidge

For the Royal Court: The Changing Room (Duke
of Yorks), Wildfire (YPT tour).
Other theatre includes: Afore Night Come
(Young Vic); The Contractor (Derby Playhouse &
tour); The Riot (RNT); Henry V (RSC); Blue
Remembered Hills (Sheffield Crucible); Peter Pan
(Birmingham Rep); Under Milk Wood
(Wimbledon Studio Theatre).
Television includes: Sherlock Holmes – A Case of
Evil, Crime & Punishment, Hearts & Bones,
Tough Love, The Bill, Blind Date, All The King's
Men, Casualty, A Wing and a Prayer, Holding the
Baby, Touching Evil, The Heart Surgeon, Moll
Flanders, Six Sides of Coogan, Hetty Wainthrop
Investigates, Pie in the Sky, Frontiers, Band of
Gold, Eastenders.
Film includes: Bridget Jones' Diary, East is East,
Shakespeare in Love, Keep the Aspidistra Flying,
The Man Who Knew Too Little, The English
Patient.

Ian Rickson (director)

Ian Rickson is Artistic Director of the Royal
Court.
For the Royal Court: Boy Gets Girl, Mouth To
Mouth (& Albery), Dublin Carol, The Weir
(Theatre Upstairs, Theatre Downstairs &
Broadway), The Lights, Pale Horse, Mojo (&
Steppenwolf Theatre, Chicago), Ashes and Sand,
Some Voices, Killers, 1992 Young Writers'
Festival, Wildfire.
Other theatre includes: The Day I Stood Still
(RNT); The House of Yes (The Gate): Me and
My Friend (Chichester Festival Theatre); Queer
Fish (BAC); First Strike (Soho Poly).
Opera includes: La Serva Padrona (Broomhill).

Paul Ritter

For the Royal Court: Bluebird (Young Writers
Festival 1998).
Other theatre includes: Howard Katz,
Remembrance of Things Past, All My Sons
(RNT); Troilus and Cressida, Three Sisters
(Oxford Stage Company); Drummers (Out of
Joint); Belle Fontaine (Soho); The Overcoat (The
Clod Ensemble); Snake in the Grass (Peter Hall
Co); Happy Valley (Liverpool Everyman); Troilus
and Cressida, The White Devil, Three Hours

After Marriage (RSC); Grimm Tales (Leicester
Haymarket); Grab the Dog (RNT Studio);
Crossing the Equator, Raising Fires, Darwin's
Flood (Bush); Time and The Room, The Great
Highway, Seven Doors (Gate); An Evening With
Gary Lineker (Colchester).
Television includes: Fields of Gold, Big Cat, Out
of Hours, The Bill, National Achievement Day,
Seaforth, Small Change.
Film includes: Joyrider I, Esther Kahn, The Nine
Lives of Tomas Katz, Greenwich Mean Time.
Radio includes: Water, The Magpie Stories, Kill
the Cameraman First, Ruby on Tuesday, Five
Letters Home to Elizabeth, The Vagabond,
Murder on the Home Front, The Deep Blue Sea,
Thrush Green, Agent 52, Grease Monkeys, Skin
Deep.

Finlay Robertson

Theatre includes: The Alchemist (Riverside
Studios): Scream if You Want To Go Faster
(Unlimited Theatre); Play With Me (Camden
People's Theatre); Duchess of Malfi (Barons
Court Theatre & The Prince Theatre); Weepie
(Edinburgh Fringe); Kissing Bingo (Edinburgh
Fringe & The Finborough Arms); The Tempest
(Selected Domestic Locations); Death of a
Salesman, Antony & Cleopatra (ADC Theatre);
Jew of Malta (ADC Theatre & Edinburgh Fringe).
Television includes: Lexx, Talk To Me, Cry Wolf,
Peak Practice.
Film includes: Eye Candy, Nice, The
Inbetweeners, The Mild Bunch, The Truth Is,
Creamachine, Never Better, Happy End, It's
Nice To Go Trav'lin, Isacek.

Jessica Stevenson

Theatre includes: Blithe Spirit (Theatre Royal,
York); Fiddler on the Roof, The Plough & The
Stars, Brighton Rock (West Yorkshire Playhouse);
The Caucasian Chalk Circle, Surrender Dorothy,
Blood Wedding (National Youth Theatre); Blitz!
(Playhouse Theatre); The Rivals (Greenwich &
Theatre Royal, Brighton).
Television includes: Spaced (which Jessica co-
wrote); Bob and Rose, House of Eliott, Tears
Before Bedtime, Crown Prosecutor, 6 Pairs of
Pants, Asylum, The Midsomer Murders, Staying
Alive, Barking, Armstrong & Miller, The Royle
Family (4 series), Harry Enfield Christmas
Special, The Paul Kaye Sketch Show, Randall &
Hopkirk Deceased, People Like Us.
Film includes: Swing Kids, The Baby of Macon,
The Sweeny.
Awards includes: The Best Female Comedy
Newcomer in 2001 British Comedy Awards.
Jessica was nominated Best Actress in the
Comedy Awards 2001 for her performances in
The Royle Family, Bob & Rose and Spaced.

Ray Winstone

For the Royal Court: Pale Horse, Some Voices.
Other Theatre includes: To The Green Fields
Beyond (Donmar); Dealer's Choice (RNT &
Vaudeville); Mr Thomas, Hinkerman (Old Red
Lion); QR's & Al's Clearly State (King's Head,
Islington); What A Crazy World We're Living In
(Theatre Royal, Stratford East).
Television includes: Lenny Blue, Tough Love,
Last Christmas, Births, Marriages and Deaths,
Our Boy, Kavanagh Q.C., The Ghost Busters of
East Finchley, The Negotiator, Murder Most
Horrid, Get Back I & II, Black & Blue, Birds of a
Feather, Underbelly, Paint, Absolute Hell, Mr
Thomas, Palmer, Blore, Robin of Sherwood, A
Fairly Secret Army, The Lonely Hearts Kid, Fox,
Sunshine Over Brixton.
Film includes: Ripley's Game, Last Orders,
There's Only One Jimmy Grimble, Sexy Beast,
Five Seconds To Spare, Fanny & Elvis, The
Mammy, The War Zone, Final Cut, Woundings,
Dangerous Obsession, The Sea Change, Martha
Meet Frank, Daniel & Laurence, Face, Yellow,
Nil By Mouth, Ladybird Ladybird, Tank Mailling,
All Washed Up, Quadrophenia, Scum, That
Summer.
Awards include: BAFTA nomination for Best
Drama Serial and Broadcast Award for Best
Drama 2000 for Births, Marriages and Deaths.
BIFA Award for Best Male Actor in Nil By
Mouth and Europen Film Award nomination for
Best Male Actor in The War Zone 1999. RST
Award 1998 for Best Male Actor in Our Boy
and a BAFTA nomination for Best Male Actor in
Nil by Mouth 1997.

Ultz (designer)

For the Royal Court: Fireface, Lift Off, Mojo.
Other theatre includes: As designer: 16
productions for the RSC including Good (also
on Broadway), The Art of Success (also
Manhattan Theatre Club). Happy as a Sandbag,
The Black Prince, Me and Mamie O' Rourke, A
Madhouse in Goa, Animal Crackers (West End);
Slavs! (Hampstead); Arturo Ui, Ramayana
(RNT); Mojo (Steppenwolf Theater Company,
Chicago); Xerxes, La Clemenza di Tito, The
Rake's Progress (Bavarian State Opera).
As director and designer: Summer Holiday
(Blackpool Opera House, London Apollo, UK
tour, South African tour); Jesus Christ Superstar
(Aarhus and Copenhagen); Don Giovanni, Cosi
fan tutte (in Japanese for Tokyo Globe); A
Midsummer Night's Dream (National Arts
Centre, Ottawa); Dragon (RNT); The Screens
(California); The Maids, Deathwatch (co-
directed RSC); The Blacks (co-directed Market
Theatre Johannesburg and Stockholms
Stadsteater); Perikles (Stockholms Stadsteater);
Snowbull (Hampstead); The Public, The Taming
of the Shrew, Pericles, Baiju Bawra (Theatre
Royal, Stratford East, where he is now an
Associate Director).

Stephen Warbeck (composer)

For the Royal Court: Boy Gets Girl, Mouth To
Mouth, The Glory of Living, The Lights, Harry
and Me, Pale Horse, Rat in the Skull, Mojo,
Simpatico, Some Voices, The Editing Process,
The Kitchen, Blood, Greenland, Bloody Poetry,
A Lie of the Mind, Built on Sand.
Other theatre includes: The Prime of Miss Jean
Brodie, The Day I Stood Still, Light Shining in
Buckinghamshire, An Inspector Calls, Machinal,
The Mother, Roots, Magic Olympical Games, At
Our Table (RNT); The Tempest, Romeo and
Juliet, The White Devil, The Taming of the
Shrew, The Cherry Orchard, Cymbeline (RSC);
To The Green Fields Beyond (Donmar).
Television includes: A Christmas Carol, Bright
Hair, The Student Prince, Element of Doubt,
Truth or Dare, Meat, Nervous Energy, Prime
Suspect, In the Border Country, Roots, Nona,
You, Me and Marley, Happy Feet, Bitter
Harvest, The Changeling, Skallagrigg.
Film includes: Birthday Girl, Deséo, Charlotte
Gray, Captain Corelli's Mandolin, Gabriel and
Me, Billy Elliot, Quills, Very Annie Mary,
Mystery Men, Fanny and Elvis, Shakespeare In
Love, Heart, My Son the Fanatic, Mrs Brown,
Different For Girls, Brothers in Trouble, O
Mary This London, Sister My Sister.
Awards include: Academy Award and BAFTA
Nomination for Best Original Musical or
Comedy Score for Shakespeare in Love.
Stephen has also written music for many BBC
Radio plays and writes for his band the
hKippers and also for The Metropolitan Water
Board.

THE ENGLISH STAGE COMPANY
AT THE ROYAL COURT

The English Stage Company at the Royal Court opened in 1956 as a subsidised theatre producing new British plays, international plays and some classical revivals.

The first artistic director George Devine aimed to create a writers' theatre, 'a place where the dramatist is acknowledged as the fundamental creative force in the theatre and where the play is more important than the actors, the director, the designer'. The urgent need was to find a contemporary style in which the play, the acting, direction and design are all combined. He believed that 'the battle will be a long one to continue to create the right conditions for writers to work in'.

Devine aimed to discover 'hard-hitting, uncompromising writers whose plays are stimulating, provocative and exciting'. The Royal Court production of John Osborne's Look Back in Anger in May 1956 is now seen as the decisive starting point of modern British drama and the policy created a new generation of British playwrights. The first wave included John Osborne, Arnold Wesker, John Arden, Ann Jellicoe, N F Simpson and Edward Bond. Early seasons included new international plays by Bertolt Brecht, Eugène Ionesco, Samuel Beckett, Jean-Paul Sartre and Marguerite Duras.

The theatre started with the 400-seat proscenium arch Theatre Downstairs, and then in 1969 opened a second theatre, the 60-seat studio Theatre Upstairs. Some productions transfer to the West End, such as Caryl Churchill's Far Away, Conor McPherson's The Weir, Kevin Elyot's Mouth to Mouth and My Night With Reg. The Royal Court also co-produces plays which have transferred to the West End or toured internationally, such as Sebastian Barry's The Steward of Christendom and Mark Ravenhill's Shopping and Fucking (with Out of Joint), Martin McDonagh's The Beauty Queen Of Leenane (with Druid Theatre Company), Ayub Khan-Din's East is East (with Tamasha Theatre Company, and now a feature film).

Since 1994 the Royal Court's artistic policy has again been vigorously directed to finding and producing a new generation of playwrights. The writers include Joe Penhall, Rebecca Prichard, Michael Wynne, Nick Grosso, Judy Upton, Meredith Oakes, Sarah Kane, Anthony Neilson, Judith Johnson, James Stock, Jez Butterworth, Marina Carr, Simon Block, Martin McDonagh, Mark Ravenhill, Ayub Khan-Din, Tamantha Hammerschlag, Jess Walters, Che Walker, Conor McPherson, Simon Stephens, Richard Bean, Roy

photo: Andy Chopping

Williams, Gary Mitchell, Mick Mahoney, Rebecca Gilman, Christopher Shinn, Kia Corthron, David Gieselmann, Marius von Mayenburg, David Eldridge, Leo Butler, Zinnie Harris, Grae Cleugh, Roland Schimmelpfennig and Vassily Sigarev. This expanded programme of new plays has been made possible through the support of A.S.K Theater Projects, the Jerwood Charitable Foundation, the American Friends of the Royal Court Theatre and many in association with the Royal National Theatre Studio.

In recent years there have been record-breaking productions at the box office, with capacity houses for Jez Butterworth's Mojo, Sebastian Barry's The Steward of Christendom, Martin McDonagh's The Beauty Queen of Leenane, Ayub Khan-Din's East is East, Eugène Ionesco's The Chairs, David Hare's My Zinc Bed and Conor McPherson's The Weir, which transferred to the West End in October 1998 and ran for nearly two years at the Duke of York's Theatre.

The newly refurbished theatre in Sloane Square opened in February 2000, with a policy still inspired by the first artistic director George Devine. The Royal Court is an international theatre for new plays and new playwrights, and the work shapes contemporary drama in Britain and overseas.

REBUILDING THE ROYAL COURT

In 1995, the Royal Court was awarded a National Lottery grant through the Arts Council of England, to pay for three quarters of a £26m project to completely rebuild its 100-year old home. The rules of the award required the Royal Court to raise £7.6m in partnership funding. The building has been completed thanks to the generous support of those listed below.

We are particularly grateful for the contributions of over 5,700 audience members.

English Stage Company Registered Charity number 231242.

ROYAL COURT DEVELOPMENT BOARD
Tamara Ingram (Chair)
Jonathan Cameron (Vice Chair)
Timothy Burrill
Anthony Burton
Jonathan Caplan QC
Deborah Davis
Cecily Engle
Kimberly Fortier
Julia Hobsbawm
Joyce Hytner
Mary Ellen Johnson
Dan Klein
Michael Potter
Mark Robinson
William Russell
Sue Stapely
James L Tanner

PRINCIPAL DONOR
Jerwood Foundation

WRITERS CIRCLE
The Cadogan Estate
Carillon/Schal
News International plc
Pathé
The Eva and Hans K Rausing Trust
The Rayne Foundation
Sky
Garfield Weston Foundation

DIRECTORS CIRCLE
The Esmée Fairbairn Foundation
The Granada Group plc

ACTORS CIRCLE
Edwin C Cohen & The Blessing Way Foundation
Sir Ronald Cohen & Sharon Harel-Cohen
Quercus Charitable Trust
The Basil Samuel Charitable Trust
The Trusthouse Charitable Foundation

The Woodward Charitable Trust

SPECIFIC DONATIONS
The Foundation for Sport and the Arts for Stage System
John Lewis Partnership plc for Balcony
City Parochial Foundation for Infra Red Induction Loops and Toilets for Disabled Patrons
RSA Art for Architecture Award Scheme for Antoni Malinowski Wall Painting

THE AMERICAN FRIENDS OF THE ROYAL COURT THEATRE

AFRCT support the mission of the Royal Court and are primarily focused on raising funds to enable the theatre to produce new work by emerging American writers. Since this not-for-profit organisation was founded in 1997, AFRCT has contributed to seven productions including Rebecca Gilman's Boy Gets Girl. They have also supported the participation of young artists in the Royal Court's acclaimed International Residency.

If you would like to support the ongoing work of the Royal Court, please contact the Development Department on 020 7565 5050.

AMERICAN FRIENDS

Founders
Harry Brown
Victoria Elenowitz
Francis Finlay
Monica Gerard-Sharp
The Howard Gilman Foundation
Jeananne Hauswald
Mary Ellen Johnson
Dany Khosrovani
Kay Koplovitz
The Laura Pels Foundation
The Magowan Family Foundation
Monica Menell-Kinberg Ph.D.
Benjamin Rauch
Rory Riggs
Robert Rosenkranz
Gerald Schoenfeld, The Shubert Organization

Patrons
Daniel Baudendistel
Arthur Bellinzoni
Miriam Bienstock
Robert L & Janice Billingsley
Catherine G Curran
Leni Darrow
Michael & Linda Donovan
Ursula & William Fairbairn
April Foley
Amanda Foreman
Mr & Mrs Richard Gelfond
Mr & Mrs Richard Grand
Mr & Mrs Paul Hallingby
Sharon King Hoge
The Carl C Icahn Family Foundation
Maurice & Jean R Jacobs
Mr & Mrs Ernest Kafka
Sahra T Lese
Susan & Martin Lipton
Eleanor Margolis

Hamish & Georgone Maxwell
Kathleen O'Grady
Howard & Barbara Sloan
Margaret Jackson Smith
Mika Sterling
Arielle Tepper
The Thorne Foundation

Benefactors
Mr & Mrs Tom Armstrong
Mr & Mrs Mark Arnold
Elaine Attias
Rachael Bail
Mr & Mrs Matthew Chapman
David Day
Richard & Rosalind Edelman
Abe & Florence Elenowitz
Hiram & Barbara Gordon
Mr & Mrs Brian Keelan
Jennifer C E Laing
Burt Lerner
Imelda Liddiard
Dr Anne Locksley
Mr & Mrs Rudolph Rauch
Lawrence & Helen Remmel
Mr & Mrs Robert Rosenberg
Mr & Mrs William Russell
Harold Sanditen
Mr & Mrs Robert Scully
Julie Talen
Mr & Mrs Charles Whitman

American Friends
Development Director
Timothy Runion
Tel: (212) 408 0465

THE ARTS COUNCIL OF ENGLAND

PROGRAMME SUPPORTERS

The Royal Court (English Stage Company Ltd) receives its principal funding from London Arts. It is also supported financially by a wide range of private companies and public bodies and earns the remainder of its income from the box office and its own trading activities.
The Royal Borough of Kensington & Chelsea gives an annual grant to the Royal Court Young Writers' Programme and the London Boroughs Grants Committee provides project funding for a number of play development initiatives.

The Jerwood Charitable Foundation continues to support new plays by new playwrights through the Jerwood New Playwrights series. Since 1993 the A.S.K. Theater Projects of Los Angeles has funded a Playwrights' Programme at the theatre. Bloomberg Mondays, the Royal Court's reduced price ticket scheme, is supported by Bloomberg.

TRUSTS AND FOUNDATIONS
American Friends of the Royal Court Theatre
Anon
The Carnegie United Kingdom Trust
Carlton Television Trust
Gerald Chapman Fund
The Dorset Foundation
The Foundation for Sport and the Arts
Genesis Foundation
The Goldsmiths' Company
Jerwood Charitable Foundation
John Lyon's Charity
The Laura Pels Foundation
Quercus Charitable Trust
The Peggy Ramsay Foundation
The Peter Jay Sharp Foundation
The Royal Victoria Hall Foundation
The Sobell Foundation
The Trusthouse Charitable Foundation
Garfield Weston Foundation

MAJOR SPONSORS
Amerada Hess
A.S.K. Theater Projects
AT&T: _OnStage_
BBC
Bloomberg
Channel Four
Lever Fabergé
Royal College of Psychiatrists

BUSINESS MEMBERS
BP
CGNU plc
J Walter Thompson
Lazard
McCABES
Pemberton Greenish
Peter Jones
Redwood
SIEMENS
Simons Muirhead & Burton

INDIVIDUAL MEMBERS
Patrons
Anon
Advanpress
Mark Bentley

Katie Bradford
Mrs Alan Campbell-Johnson
Coppard & Co.
David Day
Mrs Phillip Donald
Robyn Durie
Thomas Fenton
Ralph A Fields
John Flower
Edna & Peter Goldstein
Homevale Ltd
Tamara Ingram
Mr & Mrs Jack Keenan
Barbara Minto
New Penny Productions Ltd
Martin Newson
AT Poeton & Son Ltd.
André Ptaszynski, Really Useful Theatres
Caroline Quentin
William & Hilary Russell
Ian & Carol Sellars
Miriam Stoppard
Jan & Michael Topham
Mr & Mrs Anthony Weldon
Richard Wilson OBE
Amanda Vail

Benefactors
Anon
Anastasia Alexander
Lesley E Alexander
Mr & Mrs J Attard-Manché
Elaine Mitchell Attias
Matilde Attolico
Tom Bendhem
Jasper Boersma
Keith & Helen Bolderson
Jeremy Bond
Brian Boylan
Mrs Elly Brook JP
Julian Brookstone
Paul & Ossi Burger
Debbi & Richard Burston
Yuen-Wei Chew
Martin Cliff
Carole & Neville Conrad
Conway Van Gelder
Barry Cox
Peter Czernin
Deborah Davis
Chris & Jane Deering
Zöe Dominic
Lorraine Esdaile
Winston & Jean Fletcher
Nick Fraser

Jacqueline & Jonathan Gestetner
Michael Goddard
Carolyn Goldbart
Judy & Frank Grace
Byron Grote
Sue & Don Guiney
Woodley Hapgood
Jan Harris
Phil Hobbs
Amanda Howard Associates
Mrs Martha Hummer Bradley
Lisa Irwin-Burgess
Paul Kaju & Jane Peterson
Mr & Mrs T Kassem
Peter & Maria Kellner
Diana King
Lee & Thompson
Caroline & Robert Lee
Carole A Leng
Lady Lever
Colette & Peter Levy
Ann Lewis
Ian Mankin
Christopher Marcus
David Marks
Alan & Tricia Marshall
Nicola McFarland
Eva Monley
Pat Morton
Georgia Oetker
Paul Oppenheimer
Janet & Michael Orr
Diana Parker
Maria Peacock
Pauline Pinder
Mr Thai Ping Wong
Jeremy Priestley
Simon Rebbechi
John & Rosemarie Reynolds
Samuel French Ltd
Bernice & Victor Sandelson
John Sandoe (Books) Ltd
Nicholas Selmes
Bernard Shapero
Jenny Sheridan
Lois Sieff OBE
Peregrine Simon
Brian D Smith
John Soderquist
The Spotlight
Max Stafford-Clark
Sue Stapely
June Summerill
Anthony Wigram

George & Moira Yip
Georgia Zaris

STAGE HANDS CIRCLE
Graham Billing
Andrew Cryer
Lindy Fletcher
Susan Hayden
Mr R Hopkins
Philip Hughes Trust
Dr A V Jones
Roger Jospe
Miss A Lind-Smith
Mr J Mills
Nevin Charitable Trust
Janet & Michael Orr
Jeremy Priestley
Ann Scurfield
Brian Smith
Harry Streets
Thai Ping Wong
Richard Wilson OBE
C C Wright

LONDON ARTS

AWARDS FOR
THE ROYAL COURT

Terry Johnson's Hysteria won the 1994 Olivier Award for Best Comedy, and also the Writers' Guild Award for Best West End Play. Kevin Elyot's My Night with Reg won the 1994 Writers' Guild Award for Best Fringe Play, the Evening Standard Award for Best Comedy, and the 1994 Olivier Award for Best Comedy. Joe Penhall was joint winner of the 1994 John Whiting Award for Some Voices. Sebastian Barry won the 1995 Writers' Guild Award for Best Fringe Play, the Critics' Circle Award and the 1995 Lloyds Private Banking Playwright of the Year Award for The Steward of Christendom. Jez Butterworth won the 1995 George Devine Award, the Writers' Guild New Writer of the Year Award, the Evening Standard Award for Most Promising Playwright and the Olivier Award for Best Comedy for Mojo.

The Royal Court was the overall winner of the 1995 Prudential Award for the Arts for creativity, excellence, innovation and accessibility. The Royal Court Theatre Upstairs won the 1995 Peter Brook Empty Space Award for innovation and excellence in theatre.

Michael Wynne won the 1996 Meyer-Whitworth Award for The Knocky. Martin McDonagh won the 1996 George Devine Award, the 1996 Writers' Guild Best Fringe Play Award, the 1996 Critics' Circle Award and the 1996 Evening Standard Award for Most Promising Playwright for The Beauty Queen of Leenane. Marina Carr won the 19th Susan Smith Blackburn Prize (1996/7) for Portia Coughlan. Conor McPherson won the 1997 George Devine Award, the 1997 Critics' Circle Award and the 1997 Evening Standard Award for Most Promising Playwright for The Weir. Ayub Khan-Din won the 1997 Writers' Guild Awards for Best West End Play and Writers' Guild New Writer of the Year and the 1996 John Whiting Award for East is East (co-production with Tamasha).

At the 1998 Tony Awards, Martin McDonagh's The Beauty Queen of Leenane (co-production with Druid Theatre Company) won four awards including Garry Hynes for Best Director and was nominated for a further two. Eugene Ionesco's The Chairs (co-production with Theatre de Complicite) was nominated for six Tony awards. David Hare won the 1998 Time Out Live Award for Outstanding Achievement and six awards in New York including the Drama League, Drama Desk and New York Critics Circle Award for Via Dolorosa. Sarah Kane won the 1998 Arts Foundation Fellowship in Playwriting. Rebecca Prichard won the 1998 Critics' Circle Award for Most Promising Playwright for Yard Gal (co-production with Clean Break).

Conor McPherson won the 1999 Olivier Award for Best New Play for The Weir. The Royal Court won the 1999 ITI Award for Excellence in International Theatre. Sarah Kane's Cleansed was judged Best Foreign Language Play in 1999 by Theater Heute in Germany. Gary Mitchell won the 1999 Pearson Best Play Award for Trust. Rebecca Gilman was joint winner of the 1999 George Devine Award and won the 1999 Evening Standard Award for Most Promising Playwright for The Glory of Living.

Roy Williams and Gary Mitchell were joint winners of the George Devine Award 2000 for Most Promising Playwright for Lift Off and The Force of Change respectively. At the Barclays Theatre Awards 2000 presented by the TMA, Richard Wilson won the Best Director Award for David Gieselmann's Mr Kolpert and Jeremy Herbert won the Best Designer Award for Sarah Kane's 4.48 Psychosis. Gary Mitchell won the Evening Standard's Charles Wintour Award 2000 for Most Promising Playwright for The Force of Change. Stephen Jeffreys' I Just Stopped by to See The Man won an AT&T: On Stage Award 2000. David Eldridge's Under the Blue Sky won the Time Out Live Award 2001 for Best New Play in the West End. Leo Butler won the George Devine Award 2001 for Most Promising Playwright for Redundant. Roy Williams won the Evening Standard's Charles Wintour Award 2001 for Most Promising Playwright for Clubland. Grae Cleugh won the 2001 Olivier Award for Most Promising Playwright for Fucking Games.

In 1999, the Royal Court won the European theatre prize New Theatrical Realities, presented at Taormina Arte in Sicily, for its efforts in recent years in discovering and producing the work of young British dramatists.

ROYAL COURT BOOKSHOP

The bookshop offers a wide range of playtexts and theatre books, with over 1,000 titles. Located in the downstairs Bar and Food area, the bookshop is open Monday to Saturday, afternoons and evenings.

Many Royal Court playtexts are available for just £2 including works by Harold Pinter, Caryl Churchill, Rebecca Gilman, Martin Crimp, Sarah Kane, Conor McPherson, Ayub Khan-Din, Timberlake Wertenbaker and Roy Williams.

For information on titles and special events, Email: bookshop@royalcourttheatre.com
Tel: 020 7565 5024

FOR THE ROYAL COURT

ARTISTIC
Artistic Director **Ian Rickson**
Assistant to the Artistic Director **Jo Luke**
Associate Director **Dominic Cooke**
Associate Director International **Elyse Dodgson**
Associate Director Casting **Lisa Makin**
Associate Directors* **Stephen Daldry, James Macdonald, Katie Mitchell, Max Stafford-Clark, Richard Wilson**
Literary Manager **Graham Whybrow**
Literary Associate **Stephen Jeffreys***
Voice Associate **Patsy Rodenburg***
Casting Assistant **Amy Ball**
International Administrator **Ushi Bagga**
International Associate **Ramin Gray**
International Assistant **Rachel Toogood**
Resident Dramatist **Roy Williams**

YOUNG WRITERS' PROGRAMME
Associate Director **Ola Animashawun**
Administrator **Nina Lyndon**
Outreach Worker **Lucy Dunkerley**
Writers Tutor **Simon Stephens***
Administrative Assistant **Lorna Rees**

PRODUCTION
Production Manager **Paul Handley**
Deputy Production Manager **Sue Bird**
Facilities Manager **Fran McElroy**
Facilities Deputy **Adair Ballantine**
Production Assistant **Jane Ashfield**
Company Stage Manager **Cath Binks**
Head of Lighting **Johanna Town**
Assistant Electricians **Gavin Owen, Andrew Taylor**
Lighting Board Operator JTD **Richard Wright**
Head of Stage **Martin Riley**
Stage Deputy **Steven Stickler**
Stage Chargehand **Daniel Lockett**
Acting Head of Sound **Ian Dickinson**
Sound Operator JTD **Michael Winship***
Head of Wardrobe **Iona Kenrick**
Wardrobe Deputy **Jackie Orton**

MANAGEMENT
Executive Director **Barbara Matthews**
Assistant to the Executive Director **Nia Janis**
General Manager **Diane Borger**
Administration Interns **Vanessa Cook, Juliette Goodman**
Finance Director **Sarah Preece**
Finance Officer **Rachel Harrison**
Finance Assistant **Martin Wheeler**
Accountant **Simone De Bruyker***

MARKETING & PRESS
Head of Marketing **Penny Mills**
Head of Press **Ewan Thomson**
Marketing Officer **Charlotte Franklin**
Marketing and Press Assistant **Claire Christou**
Box Office Manager **Neil Grutchfield**
Deputy Box Office Manager **Valli Dakshinamurthi**
Duty Box Office Manager **Glen Bowman**
Box Office Sales Operators **Carol Pritchard, Steven Kuleshnyk**

DEVELOPMENT
Head of Development **Helen Salmon**
Development Associate **Susan Davenport***
Sponsorship Manager **Rebecca Preston**
Development Officer **Alex Lawson**
Development Assistant **Chris James**
Development Intern **Vangel Efthimiadou**

FRONT OF HOUSE
Theatre Manager **Elizabeth Brown**
Duty House Manager **Suzanne Kean, Paul McLaughlin, Neil Morris***
Bookshop Manager **Peggy Riley**
Assistant Bookshop Manager **Simon David**
Bookshop Assistants **Michael Chance, Jennie Fellows, Suzanne Kean**
Stage Door/Reception **Hannah Caughlin, Simon David, Kelda Holmes, Hannah Lawrence, Tyrone Lucas, Andrew Pepper, Kathleen Smiley**
Thanks to all of our ushers

* part-time

THE NIGHT HERON

for
John Butterworth
1924–99

Characters

JESS WATTMORE

GRIFFIN

BOLLA FOGG, *a woman*

NEDDY BEAGLE

ROYCE

DOUGAL

JONATHAN, *a student*

A BIRDWATCHER

SON *of the birdwatcher*

*The play is set in the Cambridgeshire fens, in the New Year,
over a few short, freezing days*

ONE

*Darkness. Local fenland radio. A farm auction. A church fete.
Rising seas. A poetry competition for short verse, organised
by Cambridge University. The first prize is £2,000. The closing
date is in two weeks. Wind. Gull and tern cry out. A man's*
VOICE *on a tape.*

VOICE. And the Lord God planted a garden eastward in Eden.
And out of the ground made the Lord God to grow every
tree that is pleasant to the sight, and good for food; the tree
of life also in the midst of the garden, and the tree of
knowledge of good and evil.

A penny whistle plays.

*A cabin, built from ship timber a hundred years ago. Strip
plastic hangs in a doorway downstage right. A door upstage
left, to an offstage lean-to bedroom. Dominating the cabin
is a giant frieze depicting Christ and the Saints. Photocopied
onto many sheets of paper, it is pinned together with
drawing-pins.*

*A coal-burning stove. Church pews for chairs. A tallboy.
On a table, a large, silver ghetto blaster.*

VOICE. And the Lord God took the man, and put him into the
Garden of Eden to dress it and to keep it. And the Lord God
commanded the man, saying: Of every tree of the garden
thou mayest freely eat. But of the tree of the knowledge
of good and evil, thou shalt not eat of it: for in the day that
thou eatest thereof thou shalt surely die.

*Sudden banging, off. Shouts. Barking. The shatter of glass.
It fades. The voice continues on the tape. Enter* WATTMORE.
*He appears from the back room in housecoat and striped
pyjamas. He has been beaten. He drinks from the galley tap,
and spits and coughs, as if coughing teeth and blood. The
tape continues. He lights a lantern, then sits at the table,
and presses play and record. He speaks low, from memory.*

WATTMORE. And the Lord said unto Adam: Because thou
hast hearkened unto the voice of thy wife, and hast eaten of
the tree, of which I commanded thee, saying, Thou shalt not
eat of it: cursed is the ground for thy sake; in sorrow shalt
thou eat of it all the days of thy life; in the sweat of thy face
shalt thou eat bread, till thou return unto the ground; for out
of it wast thou taken: for dust thou art, and unto dust shalt
thou return.

*He removes a penny whistle from his housecoat pocket and
plays a short refrain.*

And the Lord God sent him forth from the Garden of
Eden, to till the ground from whence he was taken. So he
drove out the man; and he placed at the east of the garden
Cherubims, and a flaming sword which turned every way,
to keep . . . to keep . . . to keep the way of the tree of life.

Refrain.

*He presses stop. It starts to rain. He turns the radio on –
Gardeners' Question Time – and starts rooting through the
tallboy drawers. He finds what he is looking for: a rope.
The rain falls harder as he pulls up a chair in the centre
of the cabin. He stands on it. He slings the rope over a
low beam. He ties it around his neck, and stands there,
sweating, willing himself to take the step. Offstage, a lock
turns. Someone taking his boots off in the porch.*

VOICE (*off*). Wattmore! There's a competition. For poetry at
the University. It's open to all-comers. There's a prize.
(*Stops.*) Dear oh dear. Dear oh dear oh dear. Wattmore?
There's broken glass out here. Someone's had an accident.
Dear oh dear oh dear.

WATTMORE *takes his neck out of the noose, and gets off
the stool. He just manages to throw his housecoat over the
ghettoblaster, before* GRIFFIN *enters, soaking, with two
bags of chips. He makes straight for the stove and opens it,
working the flame.*

GRIFFIN. I say there's glass all over. The porch is knackered.
Why don't you put the clicker on after you? The wind can't

get round it, whip it open smash it to buggery. It's freezing in here Wattmore. It's colder than a witch's tit.

He takes off his hat.

Let's see. That's ten pound for the pane, never you mind about labour. Congratulations. That's twenty, thirty pound, down the sink.

GRIFFIN *makes straight for the stove and opens it, working the flame.*

There's nothing out there. Right up the church back to the road, nothing. Not one. I thought I had one, in the reed beds, I've got the torch on him. But he's twiced me. So I thought stuff this. Went into town got chips.

He drops a portion on the table in front of WATTMORE, *switches off the wireless, takes his coat off, sits down, closes his eyes. A whisper:*

For what we are about to receive may the Lord make us truly thankful. For Jesus Christ's Sake. Amen.

Eats.

Bugle's still on about that bird. It's front page news. They're offering a hundred pound for a photograph. *A hundred pound.* I thought I saw him, though. Thought I had him, in the reed beds. He's soared right over, low mind, low enough to touch. But it weren't him. It was a seagull. Or a crow.

Eats.

There's a story in the *Bugle* too, one of them, the newcomers, birdwatcher it was, he's out last night on the Marsh, he's lost the path. He's fallen in a suckpit, he's kicked and kicked and it's dragged him under. He'd be dead, but he was with another had a mobile phone. He's in the hospital. Honestly, if that bird knew half the trouble he's causing.

Eats.

Did I say? There's a competition. You write a poem, and if you win they give you a prize. Wait for it. It's two thousand pound. Two thousand pound for one poem. Open

to all-comers. What do you think to that eh? What do you
think to that?

WATTMORE. He came here.

GRIFFIN. What? Who? Who came here?

Beat.

When?

WATTMORE. He was banging. And swearing. He smashed the
porch.

Beat.

GRIFFIN. Swearing?

WATTMORE. Shouting. Shouting and swearing. He had a
hound.

GRIFFIN. Right. See that's not him. Barking you say? See
that's not him. See he doesn't have a hound. He doesn't
keep one. Point of fact he can't stand 'em.

WATTMORE. How do you know?

GRIFFIN. Because.

WATTMORE. Because what?

GRIFFIN. Just Because.

WATTMORE. Because *what*?

GRIFFIN. Because he killed Black Bob's dogs.

Beat.

When Black Bob owed him that fifty pound.

WATTMORE. What?

GRIFFIN. The long version, see, if you want it, Black Bob's
bitch has just had a litter and Black Bob's in the garden at
the Plough selling the pups. He wants two pound a pup see.
Anyway he starts drinking starts betting Floyd at boules.
Now Floyd's bloody good at boules. Ten minutes Black
Bob's into Floyd for twenty five puppies. He's only got six.
Floyd spends all week asking Black Bob for the twenty five

pups or the fifty pound, doesn't mind which. Black Bob
starts avoiding him, starts drinking in the Earl of Great
Gloucester. So Floyd goes over the Earl of Great Gloucester
asks Black Bob for the fifty pound. Black Bob fobs him off
starts staying in renting videos. Floyd goes round Black
Bob's house asks Black Bob's wife for the fifty pound. She
says Black Bob's in the bath. In the end Floyd gets hacked
off. So he poisoned his puppies.

WATTMORE. Floyd poisoned Black Bob's dogs?

GRIFFIN. Yes. No. He poisoned the *puppies*. He beat the bitch
stone dead with a cricket bat.

Beat.

So.

WATTMORE. So what?

GRIFFIN. So it's safe to assume that Floyd's no great dog
lover. You heard barking. Ergo, it's not him. Be kids. Be
kids, or the wind.

WATTMORE. It weren't the wind.

GRIFFIN. Be kids then. Shouting and barking. Kids love
shouting. And kids love dogs. And dogs love barking.
How's your chips?

WATTMORE. Where've you been?

GRIFFIN. I've been out on the marsh.

WATTMORE. You've been out all day. Where've you been?

GRIFFIN. Well let's see. I went over Fen Drayton say Happy
New Year to Royce. Prat's still got his Christmas tree up.
Then I flagged down the mobile library, on Over Road. And
they had a poster up on the door. Two thousand pound it
said for one poem. So I cycled over Cambridge. And it's
true. It's on all the boards.

WATTMORE. You went to Cambridge.

GRIFFIN. I just said I did.

WATTMORE. Did you go into the college?

GRIFFIN. Now Wattmore –

WATTMORE. Did you go into Corpus Christi?

GRIFFIN. I may have. I'm welcome to. The college is open to visitors between nine and dusk week days twelve thirty to three Saturdays and Sundays –

WATTMORE. *Did you go in the garden?*

Pause.

GRIFFIN. No. I didn't go in the garden. I'm not stupid Wattmore. Grant me *some* noodles.

Pause.

Bumped into Old Ben though. On his bike, riding over the backs. Says the frost took most of those rose bushes. And the old quince tree's died. He's off to King's College in the Spring; they're moving the Master's orchard or something. An orchard might be nice. In the Spring. By the way I've been thinking about what you said, and you're right.

WATTMORE. What?

GRIFFIN. I think we should take a lodger.

WATTMORE. What? I never said we should take a lodger.

GRIFFIN. Yes you did.

WATTMORE. When.

GRIFFIN. The other day.

WATTMORE. What other day?

GRIFFIN. A month or two ago. A few months back. I think it's a good idea.

WATTMORE. But –

GRIFFIN. I do. So I put an advert in the *Bugle*.

WATTMORE. Hang on. What? Don't we discuss this? No way. Don't we discuss this? No bloody way. Where would we put them?

GRIFFIN. In there.

WATTMORE. I sleep in there.

GRIFFIN. Cushions then. A line of cushions. Over there.

WATTMORE. A line of cushions. Did you put that in the
Bugle? 'For rent, *a line of cushions.*'

WATTMORE *winces*.

GRIFFIN. What would you miss? All this quality time on
your own? You're sat here in your podgers morning noon
and night, three weeks now, you don't wash, you let the
stove go out. I'm out there looking for work. Searching the
marsh in the pissing rain for rabbits. This isn't *Summer
Holiday,* Wattmore. We need to tighten our belts. It's a
New Year, and we've got no coal. (*Pause.*) Did you get
your dole money?

WATTMORE *nods*.

Good. You owe me three pounds twenty.

WATTMORE. Why?

GRIFFIN. It's twenty-five pence a word for *Bugle* Classifieds.
If we go Dutch, and double Dutch on the chips is three
pound twenty. Call it three pound for cash. (*He puts his
hand out.*)

WATTMORE. I haven't got it.

GRIFFIN. What?

WATTMORE. I haven't got it.

GRIFFIN. I thought you said you got it.

WATTMORE. I did.

GRIFFIN. Well where is it?

WATTMORE. I haven't got it. I gave it to someone.

GRIFFIN. Who?

WATTMORE. Why should I tell you?

GRIFFIN. Who did you give it to?

WATTMORE. I gave it to Dougal.

GRIFFIN. Dougal who? Dougal who? *Dougal*? You gave –
Dougal? You gave it to *Dougal*?

WATTMORE. There.

GRIFFIN. I don't know what to say.

Beat.

Why did you give it to Dougal?

WATTMORE. He's a good man.

GRIFFIN. Jess. He's a mongol. His mother's a mongol.

WATTMORE. He's not. She's not.

GRIFFIN. Jess. I don't know everything, but Dougal and his
entire breed are mongols. They're mongol children. All the
Duggans are half-breeds. It's public knowledge. I was at
school with four of them. They hiked them out of your
class. They stuck them in a hut down the end of the field
gave them *padded desks*.

WATTMORE. Not Dougal.

GRIFFIN. Jess . . . Dougal . . . Jess. Okay. Dougal Duggan
smeared shit all over the walls of the school changing rooms.

WATTMORE. He's changed.

GRIFFIN. He's not changed. He's gone in there and smeared
shit all over the shop. Jess . . . right. For instance . . .
Dougal's mum. Dougal's mum came up the school and
hacked her tit open. Her own tit. They're all of them circus
freaks. They want to be in the circus.

WATTMORE. He's a good man.

GRIFFIN. I'm out chasing rabbits, you're giving your dole
away to mongols.

WATTMORE. He's got me work.

GRIFFIN. What work?

WATTMORE. I'm not telling you. He said I'm a flagship. Yes.
And I could work in his office.

GRIFFIN. What office?

WATTMORE. He's getting an office. He's rented a unit. In the business park. I'm working there.

GRIFFIN. Doing what?

WATTMORE. Number crunching.

Beat.

GRIFFIN. Number crunching.

WATTMORE. Yes.

Beat.

He's got the internet. He's building a website.

GRIFFIN. Oh very flash. Very . . . for your information, Wattmore, even the mobile library's got the internet. Yes. In fact I was surfing the world web this very afternoon before you have kittens. And you who's never touched it. The Internet. I *am* impressed. Oh yes. Has he paid you?

WATTMORE. He'll be paying me . . .

GRIFFIN. What for?

WATTMORE. Lots of things.

GRIFFIN. What like?

WATTMORE. Doing his tapes.

Beat.

GRIFFIN. Bollocks.

WATTMORE. I am.

GRIFFIN. Bollocks.

WATTMORE *whips off the housecoat revealing the ghetto blaster underneath.*

Beat.

Fine. Okay Jess. For example . . . Just to say, he . . . Dougal asked me to do the tapes. Six weeks ago. At the Plough. At the Australian Night. Corks all round his hat. What happened? Eh? What happened? Nothing happened.

WATTMORE. Well it has now. It's happened.

Beat.

GRIFFIN. It sounds like quite a package.

WATTMORE. It is.

GRIFFIN. You must be very proud.

WATTMORE. I am.

Car lights go past on the road outside. WATTMORE *freezes.* GRIFFIN *stands. The noise subsides.*

GRIFFIN. Be one of them birdwatchers. See. They're going out on the marsh. See?

You jumpy clot.

Silence. WATTMORE *starts to cry.* GRIFFIN *sits watching him cry.*

WATTMORE. Forgive me *Prince.*

GRIFFIN. Eat your chips. You haven't touched them.

Beat.

Shall I get you a rabbit? Do a stew. I'll go back out there. I'll catch one no trouble.

WATTMORE. *Jesu* Light and Saviour, prince over time, heed the prayer of the bastard sinners. Light the way lamb, project to us the true path of several. Send a Guardian and light braziers . . . and mark the path through Disturbance. Display the dark path to everlasting Peace. Purge the reek of sin. Purge the reek of sin.

Silence.

I didn't do it Griffin. *I didn't do it.*

Silence.

GRIFFIN. Ssshhhh.

His breath mixes with the wind.

Blackout. Music.

*The local radio returns: a night heron has been spotted
in the area. It has never been seen in the British Isles, and
birdwatchers are coming from across Europe to try to spot
the rare creature. No-one knows why it has come.*

TWO

The cabin, at dusk. The lanterns are lit. WATTMORE *and*
GRIFFIN *stand in the middle of the room in silence. From the
back bedroom appears a woman. She is* BOLLA FOGG. *She
stands there.*

BOLLA. The mattress is damp.

GRIFFIN. Is it?

BOLLA. It's mildewy.

GRIFFIN. Needs turning I expect. Probably just needs . . . you
know. A turn.

She closes the door.

WATTMORE. I told you to turn the mattress.

GRIFFIN. Leave it.

WATTMORE. I said. I said turn the mattress. I told you to
turn it.

GRIFFIN. Jess –

WATTMORE. I told you to turn it.

GRIFFIN. I did fucking turn it.

The door re-opens. BOLLA *looks at them both.*

BOLLA. It's cold.

GRIFFIN. Right. There's a little two-bar under the bed. Get both
bars on it's roasting. Give the plug a good shake though.

She is staring at the enormous iconostasis on the wall.

GRIFFIN. Oh that.

Beat.

Where to start really? It's called uh . . .

WATTMORE. Iconostasis.

GRIFFIN. That's it. They're Icons. Saints. What it is see, an Iconostasis depicts the Lord and the Saints at the final judgment. And that's pretty much what's going on up there. It's Russian.

WATTMORE. Byzantine.

GRIFFIN. Byzantine. From the Kremlin. Jess blew it up. Not the Kremlin, the picture. He found it in the mobile library took it over Ely to Rymans, and blew it up. Few years back it was, now. You get used to it.

Beat.

BOLLA. Russian?

GRIFFIN. Byzantine. But we like it, don't we?

Silence. She goes back into the room.

WATTMORE. She thinks we're queer.

GRIFFIN. She does not.

WATTMORE. She does. She thinks we're homos.

GRIFFIN. She's temporary. She's a cash cow.

WATTMORE. What d'you ask for?

GRIFFIN. Guess.

WATTMORE. Twenty-five.

GRIFFIN. Forty. She's a *mug*. Here look.

He mimes milking a cow.

WATTMORE. She's in our room.

GRIFFIN. For the time being.

WATTMORE. The bog's through there.

GRIFFIN. I know where the bog is Wattmore. I have thought about this. It's short term, but for the immediate, it's going to have to be like last March.

WATTMORE. Oh for pity's sake.

GRIFFIN. What? You were the one blocked the bog. You were the one got the plunger stuck down there. I had to squat in the rain all of March. Did I complain?

WATTMORE. Yes.

GRIFFIN. Well it's the same as that . . . That was bloody ten days, pulling on the plunger. It was like the sword in the fucking stone.

WATTMORE. Did she give you a deposit? She'll break something.

GRIFFIN. She will not.

WATTMORE. She's bloody huge. She'll break the bog. I don't like it. I'm going in there.

GRIFFIN. She's got a car.

WATTMORE (*stops*). Where?

GRIFFIN. Outside. A Golf. Nineteen ninety. Hot hatch . . . four new tyres. Electric windows. What are we talking? Five, six, seven hundred at least.

WATTMORE. Griffin.

GRIFFIN. It's purple mind.

WATTMORE. Griffin –

GRIFFIN. And she'll have thrashed the suspension.

WATTMORE. Griffin!

GRIFFIN. What?

WATTMORE. It's hers.

GRIFFIN. Of course it's hers. Of course it's hers. Of course it is. Exactly. Yes. *Is it?* Is it hers? Get her relaxed, few drinks, game of Cards. Hearts. Brag. Beggar my Neighbour . . .

WATTMORE. Griffin!

Re-enter BOLLA.

BOLLA. I'll take it.

GRIFFIN. Lovely. We can fix that lock for you. And turn the mattress . . .

She shakes GRIFFIN*'s hand.*

BOLLA. Bolla. Bolla Fogg.(*To* WATTMORE.) Bolla Fogg.

GRIFFIN. He's Jess Wattmore. I'm Griffin.

BOLLA. Jess.

She shakes his hand.

Big hands.

Beat.

WATTMORE. Yes.

BOLLA. That bog's a bit rocky.

WATTMORE (*to* GRIFFIN). What did I say?

BOLLA. Do they always do that?

WATTMORE. Who?

BOLLA. The birds.

GRIFFIN. No. It's unusual. It's the marsh. The marsh calls them. They've been coming a thousand years. Crows mostly.

WATTMORE. It's Tern. Tern and Black Backs.

GRIFFIN. It's the marsh that brings them.

BOLLA. Well it is a pretty view.

GRIFFIN. Yeah. Not for much longer mind.

BOLLA. What's happening?

GRIFFIN. The sea's coming. It's rising up. Ten years time this'll all be underwater. Past Ely, ten miles flatland that way west.

WATTMORE. They don't know.

GRIFFIN. We'd be treading water right now.

WATTMORE. They don't know. Nobody knows.

GRIFFIN. Exactly. Nobody knows. So. Bolla. I'm just making a peppermint tea.

WATTMORE. *Bloody* hell –

GRIFFIN. What? Or coffee. Or tea. Normal tea. What do you like?

BOLLA. Tea. Normal tea.

GRIFFIN. Splendid. A Normal Cup Of Tea.

BOLLA. You're black and blue.

WATTMORE. What?

BOLLA. You've got bust ribs. I can tell.

GRIFFIN. He's got two broke and six bruised.

WATTMORE. He wasn't there.

GRIFFIN. There was a doctor's report. He's got three chipped teeth, a twisted knee, a broken toe and a kick right up the arse.

BOLLA. Who duffed you up?

GRIFFIN. Gypsies.

WATTMORE. We don't know.

GRIFFIN. It was gypsies.

BOLLA. They mug you?

WATTMORE. No.

BOLLA. 'N what did they want?

GRIFFIN. Who knows what gypsies want? Murderous bastards. I bet if you could read the mind of your average gypsy, you'd never leave the house.

BOLLA. I've had ribs. They're cruel. There's nothing you can do except wait.

WATTMORE. How'd you get yours?

BOLLA. Ribs? As a girl. And as a woman.

WATTTMORE: Can I ask where are you from?

BOLLA. I've been in London.

WATTMORE. Oh really? Whereabouts?

BOLLA. I've been away.

WATTMORE. Away?

BOLLA. I've been in prison. Ta.

GRIFFIN *hands* BOLLA *a cup.*

WATTMORE. Griffin?

GRIFFIN. . . . and a normal tea for Jess here . . . yes?

WATTMORE. Can I speak to you please?

GRIFFIN. What about?

BOLLA. Didn't you tell him? Didn't he tell you? I'll go right now if it bothers you. I don't blame you. I'm very up front myself.

GRIFFIN *rolls up his sleeve.*

GRIFFIN. Here look. Look. See this. Look. See?

BOLLA. What's that?

GRIFFIN. Look. Feltham. 1976. Borstal remand for boys. Six months. Hard, hard time. I was sixteen.

BOLLA. What is it?

GRIFFIN. It's my dog. Was.

BOLLA. I was gonna say Kirk Douglas. It looks like Kirk Douglas out of Spartacus.

GRIFFIN. No. It's a Labrador. Was a Labrador.

BOLLA. He dead?

GRIFFIN. She. Pippa. Nineteen seventy eight.

BOLLA. I'm sorry.

GRIFFIN. Thanks. That says Pippa but it's smudged with the years.

BOLLA. They don't live long. Dogs.

GRIFFIN. Oh. It's a different life.

BOLLA. What was you in for?

GRIFFIN. Guess. Go on. Guess. I bet you can't.

WATTMORE. Dog-fucking.

Beat.

BOLLA. I like that. What was you in for. Wham. Right in. I like you. I like you alot. Dog-fucking.

She laughs.

GRIFFIN. So. Bolla. I see you're a Golf Woman.

BOLLA. Sorry?

GRIFFIN. Your car. Hot hatch. What colour is that? Magenta? Cerise?

BOLLA. Purple.

GRIFFIN. Nice. Respray?

BOLLA. Recut.

GRIFFIN. Wise. The same effect for a fraction of the price.

BOLLA. Can I say something?

GRIFFIN. What?

BOLLA. This has got sugar in it.

GRIFFIN. Course it's got sugar in it. It's tea.

BOLLA. I don't have a sweet tooth Griffin.

GRIFFIN. You're sweet enough already Bolla.

BOLLA. Can I say something else? That bollocks won't work on me.

GRIFFIN. Right.

BOLLA. No offence. I'm not being funny. I can be sweet. I take your point. But you can't butter me up. No one can.

Beat.

I'm sorry. I really like you both. I'm just nervous. I get a
rash when I'm nervous. I've got it now.

GRIFFIN. No you haven't.

BOLLA. I have. My neck goes all red and I get pins and
needles in my hands. I've got it right now. If the hands go
the neck goes.

GRIFFIN. The neck's fine.

BOLLA. I'm sorry. It's because I really like you and I think
we could be friends. That's why I've the stingers. I'm very
pleased to be here see. I'm just nervous. I'm a good friend
to people.

GRIFFIN. I'm sure you are.

BOLLA. Also, if we become close friends, I promise you, I'll
do anything. Anything. And if we become best friends, well
that's when I'll die for you. I'll drink this.

GRIFFIN. Right. Well it's uh . . . it's good to chew the fat.

Beat.

BOLLA. I'm going to my room now. I've put both bars on and
now I'm going to have a lie down. I'm sorry about your
dog, even though it was a long time ago. I like you. I like
you alot. And I like that.(*Iconostasis.*) It looks extremely
grand.

She goes out. She comes back.

I'm turning over a new leaf.

Silence. She goes to her room. Silence.

GRIFFIN. Nice lady.

Beat.

What?

WATTMORE. I'm only going to say this once.

GRIFFIN. Jess, She's forty pounds a week.

WATTMORE. She's a villain. She's a jailbird.

GRIFFIN. She's turning over a new leaf.

WATTMORE. We don't know her.

GRIFFIN. Of course we don't know her. She's just got here.

WATTMORE. Don't play cards with her.

GRIFFIN. What? Why not? Did I say I was going to play cards
with her? Why not? Oh I see. I see . . .

WATTMORE. She could be anyone. She could be –

GRIFFIN. Could be a what? Go on.

WATTMORE. We don't know her.

GRIFFIN. Go on say it. Say it. What? Say it. She could be a
what? Go on say it.

WATTMORE. We don't know what she is . . .

GRIFFIN. Go on. Say it. She could be a demon. Isn't? Isn't it?

Car-lights track aross the room. WATTMORE *freezes.
They listen. The engine goes away. Silence.* WATTMORE
sits down.

GRIFFIN. Be the Winkle man. Coming back from the marsh.
Two stroke, see? Jumpy clot.

Silence.

So that's that. At least we can get coal now. Maybe another
lamp. Brighten up the long nights. So did you read it?

WATTMORE. Did I read what? Oh.

GRIFFIN. What did you reckon?

WATTMORE. I don't know.

GRIFFIN. What do you mean?

WATTMORE. Look I said I have no idea, okay. I don't know
poetry. I don't know any poetry.

GRIFFIN *takes a piece of paper out of his pocket.*

GRIFFIN. Close your eyes.

WATTMORE. No.

GRIIFIN: Just –

WATTMORE. I'm not closing my eyes.

GRIFFIN. Well just give it a chance. See what it conjures up.

WATTMORE *reads it again.*

WATTMORE. Oh I see. I see.

Beat.

I understood it better that time. It's extremely poor.

GRIFFIN. Give it here.

WATTMORE. I understood it better. It's very very poor. I'll tell you what it conjures up. Bugger all.

GRIFFIN. Give it back.

WATTMORE. I'll tell you what it doesn't conjure up. It doesn't conjure up two thousand pound.

GRIFFIN. How would you know? What the fuck do you know about poems?

WATTMORE. Nothing. Not the first thing. I know one thing.

GRIFFIN. What?

WATTMORE. It's for puffs. Desperate puffs.

GRIFFIN. I can win this. I know I can. It's twelve lines. Twelve. Are you saying I don't have twelve lines of poetry in me? I know what this is. I know what this is. It's St. Ignatius.

WATTMORE. No it isn't.

GRIFFIN. Yes it is. It's St. Ignatius. It's *True Gospel.* You and your fucking *True Gospel.* He's against it, you're against it.

WATTMORE. Wrong.

Beat.

Wrong. Wrong. Wrong.

GRIFFIN. St. Ignatius says poetry is wrong. St. Ignatius says dancing is wrong. St. Ignatius says stick your head in the fire.

WATTMORE. We don't have a fire.

GRIFFIN. St. Ignatius also said it's wrong to eat owls.

WATTMORE. It *is* wrong to eat owls.

GRIFFIN. It was my book, you only read it because of me, it was out on my ticket. You never even finished it. Admit it's Ignatius. Admit it. Go on. Admit it *you big Romanist pug.*

WATTMORE. Do your bloody poem.

GRIFFIN. You do your bloody tapes.

Enter NEDDY BEAGLE, *a large man.*

WATTMORE. Griffin.

GRIFFIN. What?

He turns around.

Neddy.

NEDDY. Your porch door's smashed.

GRIFFIN. Right.

Beat.

Was the wind. Raining is it?

NEDDY. Stopped. Was raining but it stopped.

WATTMORE *goes to the back of the room, where he stands by the sink.*

GRIFFIN. Right.

NEDDY. Griffin.

GRIFFIN. Neddy.

NEDDY. Jess . . .

Silence.

GRIFFIN. How's things over the gardens?

NEDDY. Same.

GRIFFIN. Right.

NEDDY. Fellow's garden caught the frost. Lost them rose
    bushes to it.

GRIFFIN. I heard that.

NEDDY. And the quince tree died.

GRIFFIN. I heard that too.

NEDDY. Shame really. Those roses was lovely in the Summer.
    Still. To be expected I suppose. Not much you can
    do . . .

WATTMORE Should have been covered.

Beat.

NEDDY. What's that Jess?

Beat.

WATTMORE. Anyone knows the first thing about English
    Summer Royals knows you need to cloche them in a frost.
    Cloches are in the greenhouse across the Library garden. .
    Someone should have fetched them and cloched the bushes.
    Then you need a piece of old carpet, and put it round the
    roots. There's loads of cuts of carpet in the garage with the
    mowers. You cloche them, carpet them, they'd be all right.
    Wouldn't be dead now.

He walks across the room.

GRIFFIN. Where you going?

WATTMORE. Get the last of the coal.

Exit WATTMORE. *Silence.*

NEDDY. Griffin.

GRIFFIN. Neddy.

NEDDY. Spoke to Floyd Fowler this morning. Was in the
    Fellow's Garden. Chopping down the old Quince.

GRIFFIN. Right.

NEDDY. Aye. He was very unhappy. Agitated.

Beat.

GRIFFIN. I can tell you Neddy, this is a storm in a tea-cup.

NEDDY. I think it's a storm in a tea-cup.

GRIFFIN. It is. It's much ado all about nothing.

NEDDY. It's snowballed, really, hasn't it?

GRIFFIN. And now Jess is assaulted on the Marsh road. Middle of the night. They beat him hard Neddy.

NEDDY. Aye was it? I was sorry to hear about that.

GRIFFIN. We have a grievance too Neddy Beagle. But we'll turn the other cheek to see an end of it.

NEDDY. Exactly.

GRIFFIN. There now.

NEDDY. That should be it now. That should be it. Except for what his boy's saying.

Pause.

All I know is something happened, and Floyd asked me to come by to present his terms.

GRIFFIN. His terms.

NEDDY. Was it, yes.

Pause.

GRIFFIN. How much does he want?

NEDDY. Well now. Let's see. He wants a thousand pound.

Pause. GRIFFIN *laughs.*

GRIFFIN. A thousand pound. A thousand pound. (*Laughs.*)

NEDDY. To compensate. To make recompense, if you like.

GRIFFIN. And what's your cut of this Neddy? Forty, fifty pound. A hundred?

NEDDY. Oh I'm just the go-between here. Just want everything to be back to normal.

GRIFFIN. I bet you do Neddy. I bet that's it.

Neddy. You go back to Floyd, and tell him this. Tell him he can whistle for it. Tell him to go back to sleep. It's a blackmail Neddy Beagle. Thou Shalt Not Bear False Witness. There's a man drowning here. And Floyd Fowler puts his foot on his head.

NEDDY. He wants justice Griffin.

GRIFFIN. He wants a thousand pounds. It's a lie. Broken ribs Neddy. A doctor's report. We're ready. We're ready when he wants to bring in the law.

NEDDY. Be no law. Floyd won't go to the coppers on account of the fact he hates them.

GRIFFIN. There then.

NEDDY. He says he'll go to the town.

Beat.

GRIFFIN. What?

NEDDY. He says he'll go to Fen Ditton. To the *Bugle*.

Beat.

And if the *Bugle* finds out the town finds out. And if the town finds out, well then it's in God's hands, I reckon.

Pause.

GRIFFIN. He said he was going to the *Bugle*.

NEDDY. Was it, yes. To the *Bugle*, then he's going in the Earl of Great Gloucester and tell all them with children. And the Plough. He said the Town has the right to know. Way I see it, it's Floyd's boy's word against yours. And Jess so recently in public trouble.

GRIFFIN. Neddy.

Beat.

I want you to go to Floyd Fowler and tell him this. Will you remember it? Good. Tell Floyd Fowler I can give him satisfaction. Tell him I'll give him satisfaction in two days.

NEDDY. How's that?

GRIFFIN. Leave this to me. I've got something I'm selling.

NEDDY. What is it? . . . what you selling?

GRIFFIN. Never you mind.

NEDDY. It might help if I knew what it was.

GRIFFIN. Never you mind. I'm taking something into Cambridge tomorrow where there's a buyer. Two days time, you return to this house, I'll have five, six hundred pound.

NEDDY. No offence Griffin, but what have you got that's worth six hundred pound.

Pause.

Is it the car. One out there? I saw her. She's okay she is. Where'd d'you come by her then?

GRIFFIN. This isn't your concern, Go-between. I'm taking it to Cambridge, I've got a buyer, I'll have six hundred pound. And within a month I'll have the balance. And that's the end of it. And Jess is a good man. He's a good man Neddy.

NEDDY. I know you Griffin. Since I was a boy.

Jess re-enters, with the coal. Silence.

NEDDY. Won't stay then. Goodnight Jess.

Silence.

What about the bird then. Heron is it?

Beat.

And there's one in the hospital already. Still, the Plough's full. Earl of Great Gloucester. People ordering Champagne in there last night. And a Mercedes in the car-park. I reckon that Bird's done Fen Ditton a favour.

Beat.

Griffin.

Beat.

Jess.

Exit NEDDY. *Silence.*

GRIFFIN. I tell you Jess. That boy went wrong in the juniors.
When he was nine he was four foot nothing and on his tenth
birthday he was six feet four. He went from treble to bass to
out the choir in a fortnight. And I'll say this of him. He's a
crap gardener. Fit to push a wheelbarrow full of horseshit
and that's about it.

WATTMORE. What did he say?

GRIFFIN. Nothing. You're a good man Jess Wattmore.
Everybody round here knows you're a good man.

WATTMORE. What does Floyd Fowler want?

GRIFFIN. Now don't you worry about that. In two days this
will all be in the past.

WATTMORE. Griffin –

GRIFFIN. Listen to me. In two days this will be past and
everything will be back like it was. We'll go into town hold
our head up. Go in the Earl of Great Gloucester stand up
straight. And by spring we'll be back in the garden. As the
Lord is my witness I swear.

WATTMORE. Griffin –

GRIFFIN. I believe you Jess Wattmore. Do you believe me?
Do you believe me as I believe you?

*They look at each other, in the half-light of the cabin.
Re-enter BOLLA.*

BOLLA. I hope you don't think this is presuming. I was just
thinking. Tomorrow night I could cook something. I could
do a housewarming.

GRIFFIN. What?

BOLLA. Or you could. You could for me. I don't mind which.

GRIFFIN. Fine.

BOLLA. Right.

GRIFFIN. Sorry?

BOLLA. Sorry, which? You or me?

Beat.

GRIFFIN. Me.

BOLLA. Really? Are you sure? I'm not presuming? That would be lovely Griffin. What are we having?

Beat.

GRIFFIN. Rabbit.

BOLLA. Rabbit.

GRIFFIN. Rabbit stew. I'll catch one and you, Jess, you can do your rabbit stew.

BOLLA. Well that's that. Jess's doing his rabbit stew. Jiminy Cricket. Rabbit stew . . . Shit. I forgot. Also I've got miniatures. I've been saving them for a special occasion. I don't want you to think I'm gobbling down your food. I'm not a ponce.

GRIFFIN. We don't think you're a ponce do we Jess.

WATTMORE. No. We don't.

Beat.

BOLLA. I'm going to bed now. I've got both bars on. It's roasting. You can come in but knock first. Just knock twice. Or . . . I know. Jess is one knock, Griffin is two knocks. Or just knock and say your name and I'll answer. Unless I'm asleep. Don't come in if I'm asleep. Right. See you tonight Jess.

WATTMORE. See you tonight Bolla.

BOLLA. See you tonight Griffin.

GRIFFIN. See you tonight Bolla.

BOLLA. Rabbit stew. We're in the country!

GRIFFIN. Yes. Yes. We are.

Blackout. Music.

THREE

The cabin at night. A table has been set by the stove, which is roaring. BOLLA *and* GRIFFIN *have just finished eating.* WATTMORE *stares out onto the marsh.*

BOLLA. So how do you catch one?

GRIFFIN. You set a trap. A snare. You need a steel loop and they stick their head in. Now. If they stopped still they'd be fine. But Nature takes over, see, and they struggle, they try to flee. It's when you try to escape that it does for you. It just tightens and tightens till it rings your neck. That's it.

BOLLA. Right. So weren't there none out there or what?

GRIFFIN. Loads. Hundreds. Little pricks are quick as fuck though. How were your beans?

BOLLA. Lovely and hot. I don't mind my beans. I'm used to my beans. And those were Heinz. I could tell. See inside you don't get Heinz. You get some muck comes out of a sixty-gallon drum. They bulk buy. And I can't stand a bulk buy bean.

Car lights go past on the road. WATTMORE *freezes.* GRIFFIN *too. Until it passes.*

BOLLA. You not eating Jess?

GRIFFIN. His mouth's sore. It's all cut inside.

BOLLA. Does he want a painkiller? I've got temazipan.

GRIFFIN. He's just a bit quiet. He's been a bit low recently. Gets worse at night.

BOLLA. Was it the duffing up?

GRIFFIN. Yes. No. It was before the duffing up.

BOLLA. Right. That never helps though does it. Perhaps we should take him out.

GRIFFIN. No point. Town's dead as Diana in the New Year.
    There's the Earl of Great Gloucester, and the Plough.
    Plough's crap, and the Earl of Great Gloucester's full of
    birdwatchers.

BOLLA. Birdwatchers.

GRIFFIN. There's this bird that's come to the marsh see. It's
    the bird that's brought the birdwatchers.

BOLLA. What bird?

GRIFFIN. Wait. It's called . . .

WATTMORE. The night *heron.*

GRIFFIN. That's the one. Caused quite a stir. Dutch.
    Norwegians. Come over on the ferry with their dirty great
    Mercedes. If you've got a camera, you can win a hundred
    pound. You haven't got a camera have you?

BOLLA. Sorry.

GRIFFIN. Anyway, the Earl's full of birdwatchers. Are you a
    card lady Bolla?

BOLLA. What?

GRIFFIN. I just wondered if you . . . if you ever played
    cards . . .

BOLLA. No.

GRIFFIN. Oh. Little flutter now and then?

BOLLA. Never. My stepdad lived in the bookies. Kept selling
    my toys.

GRIFFIN. I see.

BOLLA. In the end I threw him out. I was twelve.

WATTMORE. It's not for everyone is it. Betting.

BOLLA. So what do you two do?

GRIFFIN. Unemployed.

BOLLA. Oh. What was you?

GRIFFIN. Gardeners. Over at the University. But not anymore. We got sacked. Well Jess got sacked and I went on strike in sympathy. And I got sacked. It's a long story. But we met in the church.

BOLLA. You churchgoers?

GRIFFIN. Used to. We don't go to church anymore. Actually we met in the cubs.

We were Scoutmasters. Fen Ditton second firsts. It's a hut round the back of the church. He was Balloo.

BOLLA. Who?

GRIFFIN. It's from *The Jungle Book*. Scoutleaders take their names from *The Jungle Book*. Arkela's a wolf. Barghera's a tiger. Balloo's a bear. He was Balloo.

BOLLA. Who were you?

GRIFFIN. I was just Griffin. They'd run out of names by then. We were Balloo and Griffin.

WATTMORE *starts collecting up his tapes. He moves his ghetto blaster.* GRIFFIN *watches him.*

But they chucked us out.

BOLLA. Why?

WATTMORE. Drop it Griffin.

GRIFFIN. Doctrinal differences. Balloo thought the cubs too worldly. He was always pushing for higher standards of devotion and cleanliness. He wanted late-night bible classes with candles. It's the cubs.

WATTMORE. Change the subject –

GRIFFIN. Asking eight-year-olds their views on *Revelations*. Poor little squirts couldn't sleep for weeks. Then he decides that someone in Brown six is in league with the devil. Warren Lee. Fucking eight years old, and a sergeant of Satan. Then one day, they've just done the Grand Howl.

BOLLA. The what?

GRIFFIN. The Grand Howl. What happens is, at the end of the pack meeting, the cubs go like this, (*He holds his arms out.*) and Barghera or someone shouts 'PACK PACK PACK'. and the cubs all shout 'PACK PACK PACK' back see, then 'AR-KAY-LA WE WILL DO OUR BEST' and then they do this (*Crouches down.*) and Arkela says, all solemn, 'Cubs, do your best and they go 'we will do our best', which is odd seeing as they've just said they would, fucking yelled it too. So anyway, it's all passed off normal when this one starts pointing at Warren Lee saying he's The Devil's last son, what have you, then he falls on the floor starts speaking in tongues. He's frothing at the mouth. Half of the sixers shat their shorts. Balloo's gone potty. I mean, it's not exactly what Baden Powell had in mind is it? It was the last straw. They threw us out. Then they threw us out of the church. Then Jess got his picture in the *Bugle*, and the University found out, and he got sacked. Which I thought was unfair, and I said so, and I got sacked.

BOLLA. That's terrible.

GRIFFIN. Yeah. But it's not all doom and gloom is it. Because now he's got Dougal.

BOLLA. Who's Dougal?

WATTMORE. Drop it Griffin.

BOLLA. Who's Dougal?

WATTMORE. Dougal's my friend.

GRIFFIN. Dougal's a mongol. His mother's a mongol. They won't let Dougal in the church either. So Dougal's setting up his own church. From his office. From his unit. In the business park. Listen to this, Bolla.

WATTMORE. That's enough –

GRIFFIN. Hang on. Listen to this. Dougal works for The Prince now but he used to work for the University as well. As a leafblower. Lowest of the low. Used to blow leaves round the University backs, and round the Fellow's garden. One day he's blowing leaves about, having a smoke, and his petrol tank on his back suddenly blows him up. He's a fireball. Burned all up his back, hideously scarred. He must look like a lizard in his Birthday suit. I'll never forget him tearing across the backs on fire, like Halley's Comet he was. Anyway, he comes out of hospital and takes the University to court. He wins twenty grand. So Dougal's suddenly rich. What does he do? Visit the pyramids? Go to Disneyland? No. He started a cult. Yes. Dougal's starts a cult. The holy son's of . . . *Son's of the White Prince.*

WATTMORE. It's not called that.

GRIFFIN. Well what is it?

WATTMORE. He hasn't decided.

GRIFFIN. It's called *The Sons of the White Prince*. Meaning the Archangel Michael. He's got this logo he's had professionally done and I *swear to Christ* it looks like Dougal on a cross. It's the Cult of Dougal. Cult of the Mongol Child. This from a boy who shat in his desk at school. And Wattmore wants to join him, don't you? He's going to work in his office. Dougal wants to harness Wattmore's powers. His power to see evil and scare the living shite out of cubs.

Dougal's told him he's a saint. He doesn't look like a saint does he, in his boots and his housecoat. That's because he's *not* a bloody saint. He's a bloody *gardener*. And he's not even that any more.

WATTMORE. Change the subject.

GRIFFIN. What? I'm just saying –

WATTMORE. Change the subject.

GRIFFIN. Change the subject. Change the subject.

GRIFFIN *gets up. He takes a roll of toilet paper out of the tall boy.*

GRIFFIN. I'll just get some more coal.

GRIFFIN *leaves, taking the coal pail on the way. They sit there in silence.*

BOLLA. Do you fancy some creme de menthe?

WATTMORE. No thanks.

Silence.

BOLLA. Any pets?

WATTMORE. What? No.

BOLLA. Me either. Had a mouse inside.

WATTMORE. Right.

BOLLA. When I was in solitary. I used to talk to it at night. And it used to talk back. You're short of company in solitary. It gets extremely lonely.

Pause.

Griffin says you've been a little 'piano' recently.

WATTMORE. What?

BOLLA. A bit low. Not yourself.

WATTMORE. Did he?

BOLLA. Anything you want to talk about?

WATTMORE. Not really.

Pause.

BOLLA. Has something happened? Apart from the cubs.

WATTMORE. No. Nothing's happened.

Pause.

BOLLA. So is Fen Ditton nice?

WATTMORE. Few shops. Earl of Great Gloucester. That's about it.

BOLLA. Right.

WATTMORE. There's the mobile library comes Mondays and Thursdays.

BOLLA. Right.

WATTMORE. And the carnival in September. And a Mayday festival. That's about it. Carnival's not bad. One year I helped pick out the Carnival queen.

BOLLA. Really?

WATTMORE. It was Jane Livingstone.

BOLLA (*shakes her head*). Sorry.

WATTMORE. She was sixteen. She had these beautiful blue eyes. We rode on the float and they had a brass band. It was in the *Bugle*. With a picture of the mayor, Jane Livingstone, and me.

BOLLA. That's nice.

WATTMORE. She's married now. The mayor said I was the type of person they could use in the town hall. Anyway it was in the *Bugle*. The other thing in the *Bugle* was all wrong. They got the wrong end of the stick.

Pause.

BOLLA. So this boy, Warren. What made you think he was a wrong un.

WATTMORE. What?

BOLLA. I just wondered. What was it you saw?

WATTMORE. I'd rather not talk about it.

BOLLA. Oh. Right. But you sensed something in him. You sensed something in him was wrong. Something was bad.

WATTMORE. You can't describe it.

BOLLA. But when someone is bad, you can tell. If someone was sitting here, for instance, in your house, you think you could tell if they were bad or not. How do you do it. Do you look into their eyes. If you look into their eyes can you see it. Can you see it?

Pause.

Can you see it Jess?

Silence. WATTMORE *is frozen staring into* BOLLA's *eyes.*

WATTMORE. What are you saying?

Pause.

BOLLA. I think it's very nice that you're showing me hospitality.

Pause.

When I first got here, I thought you and me might butt heads. But now I think different. Now I think we've got more in common than it appears initially, on the surface. Much, much more in common.

Pause.

And if you'll excuse me for a moment, Jess, I must just pop to the little girl's room.

She gets up. WATTMORE *gets up. She leaves* WATTMORE *alone. He stands there. Enter* GRIFFIN *with a pail full of coal.*

GRIFFIN. Here we go. Keep the party going. Where's she gone?

WATTMORE. We've got to get her out of here.

GRIFFIN. What? What's happened. What have you said Jess Wattmore. What have you done.

WATTMORE. I didn't do anything. What are *you* doing?

GRIFFIN. What? I'm fetching coal. What have you said to her? What did you say while I was out.

WATTMORE. Nothing.

GRIFFIN. What have you said to her?

WATTMORE. Nothing.

GRIFFIN. Wattmore . . .

WATTMORE. She had a familiar.

GRIFFIN. *What?*

WATTMORE. She had . . . she had a mouse . . .

GRIFFIN. When? What? When?

WATTMORE. She used to talk to it and it used to talk back. She said it used to talk back. We don't know what she is!

Silence.

GRIFFIN. I tell you what Jess. Why don't you ask her when she comes out? 'Excuse me, we were just wondering if you were by any chance a succubus? You know, just for the record, do you fornicate with Satan and suckle his imps?' Better still, why don't you go down the *Bugle* in the morning and tell them. I bet you a hundred pound they put you on the front page again.

WATTMORE. What are you doing telling her I was in the *Bugle*.

GRIFFIN. You were in the *Bugle*. If you weren't in the *Bugle* we wouldn't be sat here.

WATTMORE. I don't want everyone knowing it.

GRIFFIN. Everyone already knows it. It was in the *Bugle*. It was on the front page. Local Scoutleader Goes Batshit.

WATTMORE. Just shut up about it. And shut up about Dougal. And shut up about *The Sons*.

GRIFFIN. See. I told you it was called that.

WATTMORE. I'm warning you Griffin.

GRIFFIN. I didn't get us in this mess Wattmore. If you'd have not become so bloody *special* all of a sudden –

WATTMORE. Shut up.

GRIFFIN. If you'd not become so bloody *special*.

Pause.

WATTMORE. She did something.

GRIFFIN. What?

WATTMORE. She looked at me.

GRIFFIN. What do you mean.

Pause. Then:

WATTMORE. . . . her eyes . . .

Enter BOLLA. *She stands there, as if she may have heard. She enters the room.*

BOLLA. I see Griffin's back.

GRIFFIN. Yes. He is.

BOLLA. Drink?

GRIFFIN. Lovely.

BOLLA. Jess.

WATTMORE. No thank you.

Pause.

Yes. Please.

BOLLA. What have we got. Brandy. Bacardi. Frisky whisky.
You're going to get me drunk.

GRIFFIN. Steady as she goes.

BOLLA. You all right Jess. You look pale.

GRIFFIN. He's fine.

BOLLA. Are you sure?

WATTMORE. Yes.

Pause. She looks at them both.

BOLLA. So who's the bard?

GRIFFIN. Shakespeare.

BOLLA. No. I mean who's the wordsmith? Who's writing the
poems?

GRIFFIN. What?

BOLLA. There's poetry in my bathroom. On top of my bog.
It must have been there from before I moved in because
I never saw it.

GRIFFIN. Oh that's right.

BOLLA. Was it you Jess?

WATTMORE. I don't know poetry.

BOLLA. Was it you Griffin? Eh? Don't be shy.

WATTMORE. Yes.

BOLLA. Here you are.

She hands it to him.

I didn't read it. Just the first two lines. I thought it may be private. I think it's important to respect privacy. Don't you?

Pause.

So is it finished?

GRIFFIN. It's just begun. It's a work in progress.

BOLLA. What's it called?

Beat.

GRIFFIN. 'The Garden'.

BOLLA. The Garden.

GRIFFIN. Yeah.

BOLLA. What's it about?

GRIFFIN. It's about where we worked I suppose. It's about the garden in the summer. See a few years ago Jess did a mass planting in the new flowerbeds, so he went all the way to King's Lynn and spent sixty pounds of his own money on two sacks of Organite. It's Organic nitrogen fertiliser. The factory's in King's Lynn. Anyway he went and got it and he spent all week turning in the two sacks, and it really did the trick because next Mayday they all came into bloom at once. You had to see it. We had Tulip, primrose, violet, marigold, pansies, dahlia, zinnia, daisies, cockscomb, oriental lily. We were the envy of all the colleges. It was beautiful, that Summer. So yeah. Anyway. That's what it's about. It's not finished.

BOLLA. What does it represent?

GRIFFIN. What?

BOLLA. The garden. What does it represent?

GRIFFIN. Search me. It's just a garden.

BOLLA. You've got a problem.

GRIFFIN. What?

BOLLA. With the poem. With your garden.

GRIFFIN. Why?

BOLLA. It doesn't represent nothing and nothing rhymes with garden. Except harden. And Pardon. That's your lot. You could try and rhyme some of the flowers, but, see the flowers are all tough rhymes. Daffodil. Begonia. Rhododendron. It's well known. The flowers are buggers to rhyme. Plus it's already been done.

GRIFFIN. When?

BOLLA. Andrew Marvell. He did the garden in 1681. It goes

What a wondrous life I lead,
Ripe apples drop about my head,
The luscious clusters of the vine
Upon my mouth do crush their wine;
The nectarine and curious peach
Into my hands themselves do reach.
Stumbling on melons as I pass,
Ensnar'd with flowers I fall on Grass.

She stands up. She speaks the rest of the poem straight to
WATTMORE.

Such was that happy garden-state,
While man there walk'd without a mate;
After a place so pure and sweet,
What other help could yet be meet!
But 'twas beyond a mortal's share
To wander solitary there:
Two paradises 'twere in one
To live in paradise alone.

Blackout.

Interval.

FOUR

*The radio returns. It is a report about the birdwatcher in
Addenbroke's Hospital. It says the police believe he was
attacked and robbed by a masked assailant.*

*Wind. Dry, rolling thunder. Lightning. The cabin as before,
except lit by candles.* GRIFFIN *sits alone in the candlelight,
listening to the thunder. The lights in the cabin flash on and off
a few times, and then come back on.* GRIFFIN *breathes a
small sigh of relief. Enter* WATTMORE, *grim-faced, with the
toilet roll. He stows it in the tallboy.*

GRIFFIN. Maybe it's a blessing.

WATTMORE. Maybe it's not.

    WATTMORE *takes off his coat.*

GRIFFIN. We prayed didn't we. We prayed for help. Maybe . . .
I don't know. Maybe them prayers got heard.

WATTMORE. Maybe they didn't.

Silence.

GRIFFIN. Power's back on. That's a relief anyway.

WATTMORE. You shouldn't have told her about the cubs.

GRIFFIN. Look just drop it, will you. It's done.

WATTMORE. You shouldn't have told her about the *Bugle*,
you shouldn't have told her about getting the sack. You
shouldn't have told her anything.

GRIFFIN. You're sat there like a sack of spuds. I was trying to
keep the party going.

WATTMORE. Why don't you just tell her the rest? Tell her all
of it. Why don't you tell her everything?

GRIFFIN. She can help us.

WATTMORE. How? Oh for pity's sake . . .

GRIFFIN. What? She can . . .

WATTMORE. Griffin –

GRIFFIN. What? She knows it. She knows poetry.

Thunder and lightning. The lights flash and fail. Complete darkness.

GRIFFIN. That's wonderful. That's all we need. Wattmore.

WATTMORE. Dear Lord, defend this place from –

GRIFFIN. Oh stop it.

WATTMORE. Defend this place from –

GRIFFIN. Stop it Wattmore. Stop it.

WATTMORE. Defend this place from evil, drive out the fetid envious fiend –

GRIFFIN. Brilliant.

WATTMORE. . . . and leave this house for meditation of your word. Help me Prince. Help me.

GRIFFIN *strikes a match. At that moment all the lights come on.* BOLLA *is standing right in front of him. He jumps.* WATTMORE *is on his knees.*

BOLLA. There's a storm coming.

GRIFFIN. What? Yes.

BOLLA. I was on the throne and all the lights went out.

GRIFFIN. It's the storm. I'll uh . . . I'll light the candles.

BOLLA. Not to worry. If it happens again, we can pretend it's the olden days.

You all right down there Jess?

WATTMORE. I'm fine thank you Bolla.

BOLLA. Good. Good.

GRIFFIN. You know, Bolla, it's very kind of you to furnish us and all. This really is a fitting evening.

BOLLA. Thank you Griffin. That's extremely touching. I was a bit worried at first, but by this point I feel very at home.

GRIFFIN. That's because you are at home Bolla.

BOLLA. Yes. I suppose in a way I am.

She smiles.

I've been looking to settle down for a while now.

Pause.

GRIFFIN. We were just wondering Bolla. How do you know about poetry?

BOLLA. What do you mean?

GRIFFIN. Well we . . . I just wondered . . . we just were saying I wonder how she knows that.

BOLLA. Why shouldn't I?

GRIFFIN. No reason. I was just . . .

BOLLA. I don't understand the question.

GRIFFIN. No it's just, it's unusual isn't it. We don't, I don't you know . . . not many people bother with it anymore.

Pause.

BOLLA. I have studied verse.

GRIFFIN. Oh right.

BOLLA. In Holloway.

GRIFFIN. Oh I see. I see. (*To* WATTMORE.) Do you see?

BOLLA. We had options. It was an option.

GRIFFIN. Right. It was an option. Right.

BOLLA. First year was Mah Jong. Then Anatomy. Then Benchpressing. Then the Aztecs and Incas. Then verse. Some young girl, local poet, came in Saturday afternoons. She was alright but she was overly shy. She read her poems. And we read our poems. Then she got herself pregnant and never came back.

Beat.

I used to know hundreds. Me and this other girl learned
them by heart. Then I got put in solitary. When I came out
she'd gone.

GRIFFIN. There's a competition.

WATTMORE. Griffin.

GRIFFIN. What? There's a prize. You have to write one poem.

WATTMORE. Griffin –

GRIFFIN. They want one poem. That's all.

BOLLA. What's the prize?

GRIFFIN. It's one thousand pound.

BOLLA. Stone me Griffin. For verse? Who's got one thousand
for verse?

GRIFFIN. The University. Cambridge University.

She falls silent.

GRIFFIN. Are you OK Bolla?

She sits there in silence.

Did I say something wrong. Bolla. Are you . . . is
everything OK?

Silence.

BOLLA. Don't bother Griffin.

GRIFFIN. What?

BOLLA. Don't waste your time.

GRIFFIN. Why not?

BOLLA. Fucking cunts. Fucking fucking bastard fucking
cunts. Excuse my French.

GRIFFIN. What is it?

BOLLA. One Grand? They'll have a May ball, spend that on
ice. They'll roast one swan, that's a bottle of port. One
grand? They shit it. Excuse my French.

Pause.

I'm sorry, it's just I hated the place.

GRIFFIN. Oh. I see. You . . . you went to Varsity?

BOLLA. What? No. My mum worked for St. John's College. She was a bedder. You don't know what a bedder is do you Jess?

WATTMORE. No.

BOLLA. Griffin.

GRIFFIN. You bedder tell me.

Beat.

No, sorry I don't.

BOLLA. Bedder. It means some toff leaves his skidders in the middle of the floor, you have to pick 'em up. He leaves a rubber johnny swinging on the bedpost, you have to flush it for him. Because he's too busy to do it himself. He's busy off somewhere singing in Latin. In truth, he's swigging champagne in the back of a punt got his hand on some Duchess's muff. Three and six an hour for eighteen years. I'll tell you what that is. It's degrading. Call me anything. Shave my head. No-one degrades me.

GRIFFIN. Right.

BOLLA. She used to have to take me in with her, when I was a little girl. I watched toffs talk down to her. Bastard big students with their bastard big hands. Some day I'm going to go back there, and clean up for good.

Enter a policeman. BOLLA *stands straight up.*

BOLLA. Who are you?

ROYCE. Your porch is smashed.

WATTMORE. Royce.

GRIFFIN. Royce. Fucking hell. Don't you knock?

ROYCE. It's knackered. There's glass all over.

GRIFFIN. It was the wind. Don't you knock?

ROYCE. I was just on my way over Fen Ditton thought I'd drop in. How's your ribs Jess?

WATTMORE. On the mend.

ROYCE. That's good. I've been asking around. I think I'm getting to the bottom of it. I'm forming the strong opinion that it was mindless violence.

WATTMORE. I see. Well thanks anyway.

ROYCE. Who's this?

BOLLA. Who are you?

ROYCE. Who are you?

BOLLA. I asked first.

ROYCE. No you didn't.

GRIFFIN. Bolla this is Royce. Royce this is –

BOLLA. Fiona.

GRIFFIN (*beat*). Fiona. Royce this is Fiona.

ROYCE. Pleasure.

GRIFFIN. Fiona's stopped here. She's our lodger.

ROYCE. Treat to meet you Fiona. There's a storm coming.

BOLLA. Griffin. Can I have my forty pound back please?

GRIFFIN. What?

BOLLA. Can I have my forty pound back please.

GRIFFIN. Why?

BOLLA. I've changed my mind.

GRIFFIN. But . . .

BOLLA. I didn't know. That you, you know . . . that you had friends. You never said you were friends with the coppers.

GRIFFIN. What? Oh. No. (*Laughs.*) No. Royce is fine.

BOLLA. He's the coppers.

GRIFFIN. No he's not. Well, yes he is.

BOLLA. Can I have my money back please?

GRIFFIN. No. No. Royce's a mate. Aren't you Royce.

ROYCE. That's right.

BOLLA. I know. That's why I want my money back.

GRIFFIN. Look it's perfectly alright.

BOLLA. Can I have my forty pound back please Griffin, and I'll be on my way.

GRIFFIN. Excuse us.

GRIFFIN takes BOLLA downstage. Beat.

GRIFFIN. Look Bolla.

BOLLA. Fiona.

GRIFFIN. Fiona.

BOLLA. He's the coppers Griffin.

GRIFFIN. Okay. First of all, he's a bit

He makes a 'he's mad' sign.

ROYCE. I saw that.

GRIFFIN. Royce please. I'll handle this. Second of all, he's not the coppers.

BOLLA. What?

GRIFFIN. He's not the coppers. He's a Special Constable. Sounds grand doesn't it. It's not. It's not even half a copper. He's a volunteer. He does it for free.

BOLLA. Hang on. He's not the coppers? Well what's he doing dressed as the law?

GRIFFIN. That is an excellent question. He's a strimmer.

BOLLA. A what?

GRIFFIN. Strimmer. He strims the lawn edges for the University. He keeps the borders neat. He's in charge of the borders.

BOLLA. He's a gardener?

GRIFFIN. No. *We're* gardeners. *He's* a strimmer.

ROYCE. By the way I'm up for promotion Jess. I'm going to be a full Constable.

WATTMORE. Are you Royce?

GRIFFIN (*shaking his head, looking into* BOLLA*'s eyes*). 'No'.

ROYCE. Aye a month or two I'm up for my stripes. Might even get moved to Ipswich.

GRIFFIN. Again 'No'.

ROYCE. Aye I'm reading for it. I'm pages off finishing the book.

GRIFFIN. He's not finished anything. The only thing I've ever seen him finish is sandwiches.

BOLLA. I don't like coppers Griffin. I just don't like them.

GRIFFIN. Listen. He's a strimmer. It's practically fancy dress. He hasn't got the brains of a bucket of frogs.

BOLLA. He's given me the stingers. Have I gone red?

GRIFFIN. You look lovely. Relax. Sit down, and finish your ginger cake.

She sits down.

ROYCE. Your rose bushes copped it in the freeze Jess.

WATTMORE. I heard.

ROYCE. All dead. And the Quince Trees died. Floyd's chopped it down yesterday. Other than that, same. We're getting a new mower.

WATTMORE. That's nice.

ROYCE. Yeah.

Beat.

Students are back this week. And Floyd's taken on new staff. Two gyppos. Can barely speak the Queen's English. Come over in a lorry I reckon.

By the way Jess. Dougal says hello.

WATTMORE. Right. Say . . . say I say hello back.

ROYCE. He said to say he'd have come himself but he's got a meeting tonight. He was hoping you could make it.

WATTMORE. I'm still not a hundred percent.

ROYCE. We're doing God's work here in Fen Ditton. Dougal's got vision. He's got charm. He's got charisma.

GRIFFIN. He's got twenty thousand pounds.

ROYCE. What?

Beat.

What about that bloody bird then? Folks are going spare for it. I was lying in bed last night, and I thought I heard it. The question is, did it come to Fen Ditton on purpose, or has it been blown off course, by forces beyond his control. In which case, he's doomed isn't he? He'll never find his way back.

Beat.

So I was in the garden today, doing the borders, and I got talking to Floyd Fowler.

WATTMORE. Oh.

ROYCE. Strange really. He don't normally talk to me. I mean he's the gaffer. Normally he just puts two fingers up. Or gives me a nip. But this morning, he stops and starts talking to me.

WATTMORE. What did he say?

ROYCE. Well, he's not happy see.

WATTMORE. What about?

ROYCE. He's not happy with you Jess. He was warning people to stay away from you. And it's not about the cubs. He says he laid you off for a different reason. And now he's telling me to stay away from you, him that knows we're mates. He walked past us playing shove ha'penny a hundred times. Do you have any idea what he's on about.

WATTMORE. No.

ROYCE. Strange. Anyway, I thought I'd mention it.

Beat.

So have you done the tapes?

WATTMORE. Not yet. I'm doing them. Have to get the time see.

ROYCE. Have you heard him Fiona? Jess does these wondrous recorded renditions from both Old and New Testaments which he relates entirely by heart. Wondrous they are. I find them very soothing. And they really help me sleep.

WATTMORE. It's a hobby really.

GRIFFIN. Don't do yourself down Jess. It's a job. It's your job.

ROYCE. It is that.

GRIFFIN. It's a career. A profession. Your calling.

ROYCE. That's what it is. A calling. Hallelujah. You're a pure man Jess Wattmore.

GRIFFIN. Hallelujah.

ROYCE. Dougal loves you Jess.

GRIFFIN. Hallelujah. Did you hear that Jess? Dougal loves you.

ROYCE. He says he can't do it without you Jess. He says you're special.

GRIFFIN. He's not special. He's . . . OK. Enough of the bloody love in. Mutual bloody . . . What do you want Royce?

ROYCE. A quick word.

GRIFFIN. Well you've had it. Jess is very pleased to see you. Now please. Please. Just . . . Please. Go home.

ROYCE. Truth is I came to speak to you Griffin.

GRIFFIN. What about?

ROYCE. It's important.

GRIFFIN. What is it?

ROYCE. It's private.

Beat.

GRIFFIN. I see

Beat.

Fiona?

Sighs.

Fiona. Is it all right if Royce and I pop in your room for half a mo?

BOLLA. No.

Beat.

It's just you've caught me on the hop. It's just I've got all my things in there.

GRIFFIN. Okay. What if we leave the light off?

ROYCE. What?

BOLLA. No. It's my room. You can't just go in a ladies room. She might have got Ladies things in there. I'm extremely sorry. I'll tell you what? I'll go in there you can be private. I'm sorry Griffin. I'm getting prickly again. I've gone all red haven't I.

GRIFFIN. You're not red.

BOLLA. Are we still going into town? I need to lie down if we're going into town. I'm blotchy.

GRIFFIN. What yes. No. Yes. We'll see.

BOLLA. I'd like to see the sights, you know. If you still fancy. And if it'll cheer Jess up. Is that okay?

GRIFFIN. Yes. Just give me a minute.

BOLLA. Okay. I'm going to wait in here.

GRIFFIN. Lovely.

BOLLA. Okay.

She goes to the door. She comes back.

Will he be gone when I get back?

GRIFFIN. He's just leaving.

BOLLA. I hate the coppers Griffin. I'm not good with the coppers, on account of things which have happened.

GRIFFIN. I promise.

BOLLA. Thank you Griffin. I'm very happy here. If we go out later, perhaps when we get back we could put our heads together.

GRIFFIN. What?

BOLLA. We could put our heads together and work on your poem. I could give you some pointers.

GRIFFIN. Oh. Right.

BOLLA. I'll be in here. I'm very happy here.

She goes towards her room.

ROYCE. Nice to meet you Fiona.

BOLLA. What?

ROYCE. Nice to meet you.

BOLLA *disappears into the back room. Pause.*

ROYCE. Who is she?

GRIFFIN. She's no-one.

ROYCE. Is she your girlfriend? Are you . . . you know . . .

GRIFFIN. Sweet Jesus Royce.

ROYCE. Sorry. Right. Is that her car outside? Must be worth a bit. It's in pretty good nick.

WATTMORE. Would you like a drink Royce?

ROYCE. I shan't actually. I'm on duty.

WATTMORE. Right. I'm going to wash up then.

ROYCE. Right. Shall we Griffin?

They go to the front of the cabin.

ROYCE. How is he?

GRIFFIN. Who? Oh. He's the same.

ROYCE. He seems the same. Have you got to the bottom of it?

GRIFFIN. No. It's the New year. He's just a bit low.

ROYCE. I bet the beating didn't help.

GRIFFIN. No it didn't.

ROYCE. Funny. I remember last New Year he was a full of
beans. Organising the cub ramble. The Sixers and Seconders
Hike. It's like he's a different person these past few weeks.
He should get out more. We're leafleting in Ely on the
weekend. Dougal's hiring a minibus. Anyway . . .

GRIFFIN. What do you want Royce?

ROYCE. Okay, Griffin. I need your help. There's a man in the
hospital. He came to grief, out on the marsh.

GRIFFIN. Oh?

ROYCE. I'll share what I've heard. There was two out there,
a boy and his father, and they came across a man with a
balaclava. They thought it was against the cold.

Beat.

He took the man's wallet, which didn't have much in it,
and his binoculars. He even took the kiddies' packed lunch
Griffin. And his Gameboy. He robbed them with a hammer.
It was in the *Bugle* yesterday, and it's going to be in the
Bugle again in the morning.

GRIFFIN. And?

ROYCE. I just wondered if you'd seen anyone strange. You're
always out there Griffin.

GRIFFIN. I hunt in the reed beds. I stay off the marsh.

ROYCE. Right.

GRIFFIN. Everyone knows the rabbits are on the reed beds.
    Rabbits don't breed on the marsh. They don't go on the marsh.

ROYCE. I just wondered if you'd seen or heard anything out
    of the ordinary.

GRIFFIN. No.

ROYCE. Right.

GRIFFIN. Is that it?

ROYCE. Pretty much. He's going to live they think. But the
    brain is scrambled. They say he's lost his eyesight. I said
    down the station, I said it could be the Jack O'Lanterns,
    the will o'wisps, but they all laughed.

Beat.

Well goodnight Griffin. Say goodnight to Fiona for me.
Goodnight Jess.

WATTMORE. Goodnight Royce.

ROYCE. Now you get on with those tapes. It's the Prince's
    work you do now.

Beat.

You want to get that porch fixed. There's a storm coming,
and the wind's cruel tonight.

He leaves.

GRIFFIN. I don't know why you give that nicompoop the
    time of day. He thinks he's the law. He can't get his vest
    on straight.

WATTMORE. Royce said about the man. The one in the
    hospital.

GRIFFIN. What about him.

WATTMORE. He said he's blinded. He might die.

GRIFFIN. That's what he heard.

WATTMORE. I thought you said he fell in a suckpit.

GRIFFIN. So?

WATTMORE. You said you read it in the *Bugle*. You said he
  fell.

GRIFFIN. Do I work for the *Bugle* now? Am I their chief
  reporter? I skim-read it in the mobile library. I was busy
  doing . . . doing something else.

WATTMORE. It's just you said he fell.

GRIFFIN. What are you saying Wattmore? What are you
  saying? Eh? Are you saying you don't believe me. Eh? Are
  you saying that you don't believe me?

WATTMORE. Of course I believe you Griffin. Why wouldn't I?

Re-enter ROYCE.

ROYCE. I forgot to say. The scouts are having a Winter
  Wonderland in February. The Chief Constable is on the
  committee, I thought I could have a word in a few of the
  appropriate shell-likes. People forget very quickly. All can
  be redeemed, at any moment. It's never too late, when you
  think about it, is it?

Enter BOLLA. *She's wearing lots and lots of make-up, her
hair is up, and she's changed into a skirt. They all stop and
look at her.*

BOLLA. What?

She stops. She is embarrassed. Silence.

BOLLA. Are we going out Griffin? I thought we were going
  into town. I thought . . . To cheer Jess up.

They all stand there for a long time. In the end ROYCE
sniggers.

ROYCE. What's she doing . . . ?

Silence.

BOLLA. Is something funny?

ROYCE. What? Nothing's funny.

Pause.

Nothing's funny.

BOLLA. Then why are you laughing?

ROYCE. I'm not. Nothing's funny.

BOLLA. Is there a problem Griffin . . . ?

GRIFFIN. What? No. He's just leaving. Aren't you Royce.

ROYCE. Yes. Goodnight. Goodnight Fiona.

Silence.

BOLLA. Royce is it.

ROYCE. Yes.

BOLLA. Royce. Have you ever done anatomy?

ROYCE. What?

BOLLA. Have you ever done anatomy?

ROYCE. No.

BOLLA. I have. I know all about anatomy. I know loads about it. I know where your arteries are, chum.

ROYCE. What?

BOLLA. I know where your arteries are. You've got one here, one here, one here and one here. Did you know that.

ROYCE. Sorry?

BOLLA. Did you know that?

ROYCE. No.

BOLLA. It's not the biggest. The biggest is actually in your thigh. It's called the *nodal maximus* and it pumps all the blood up and down your legs and to your groin and abdomen. You learn something new every day don't you?

ROYCE. Suppose you do.

BOLLA. I can do things you wouldn't believe. You could blink and I'd be on you, see. You'd swear it wasn't happening. But it was. See that dresser. There's a knife in that drawer, for skinning rabbits. It's very sharp. You could blink once, and I'd be in there, I'd fetch it, and you'd open your eyes

and you'd be covered in blood. You'd bleed white inside
a minute. And I'll mop you up, and I'll put your fucking
corpse in the car, and drive you to the sea, and throw you
away. Now what's so funny?

ROYCE. Nothing.

BOLLA. Then why was you laughing?

ROYCE. I just thought of something funny.

BOLLA. What was it.

Pause.

ROYCE. It was something funny that happened the other day.

BOLLA. What?

ROYCE. I saw something funny.

BOLLA. What was it?

Silence.

ROYCE. It was a man. It was this man with . . .

BOLLA. With what?

ROYCE. with . . . no arms.

BOLLA. A man with no arms.

ROYCE. And a funny hat.

BOLLA. Sorry.

ROYCE. It was this man who had on a funny hat.

BOLLA. With no arms.

ROYCE. No he had arms. I was thinking of someone else.

BOLLA. So a man with a funny hat.

ROYCE. Yes.

BOLLA. Why was it funny.

Pause.

ROYCE. It had funny ear-flaps.

BOLLA. Did it?

ROYCE. Yes. It was blue. Bluey green. With funny flaps. I just
remembered it.

BOLLA. Is that true?

ROYCE. Sorry.

BOLLA. Is it true what you just said. About the funny bluey
green hat with the flaps. Is it true. And think very carefully
before you answer.

Pause.

ROYCE. No.

Pause.

BOLLA. Have you got children Royce?

ROYCE. I've got two.

BOLLA That's nice. Girls or boys?

ROYCE. Girls.

BOLLA. Two girls. There's a hammer in that drawer, and some
six inch nails. Do you want me to nail their little faces to
the floor? Right through their little eyes. Say sorry to Griffin
for bothering him tonight.

ROYCE. I'm sorry Griffin.

BOLLA. And say sorry to Jess.

ROYCE. I'm sorry Jess.

BOLLA. Good. Now apologise to Bolla.

ROYCE. Who?

BOLLA. Bolla. Apologise to Bolla.

He looks around, and throws his voice.

ROYCE. I'm sorry Bolla.

BOLLA. Say it again.

ROYCE. I'm sorry Bolla.

BOLLA. Once more.

ROYCE. I'm sorry Bolla.

Pause.

BOLLA. You're never going to come here bothering Griffin again are you.

ROYCE. No.

BOLLA. Did you walk here?

ROYCE. I'm on the bike.

BOLLA. Well get on your bike, and ride home, strimmer. Ride home to your mum.

ROYCE. Goodnight Jess.

GRIFFIN. Royce.

WATTMORE. Royce.

GRIFFIN. I'm going to speak to Dougal.

WATTMORE. Royce . . .

ROYCE. Dougal must know this. There's evil in this house.

Prince be with you. Prince be with you.

He leaves. Silence.

BOLLA. Jess, if it's all right with you, I don't think I feel like going out now. I think I'm going to get an early night.

BOLLA *goes to the drawer and she removes the hammer and a six inch nail.*

By the way, you can borrow my car, Griffin. Any time you want, if I'm not using it, just borrow the keys. All you have to do is ask.

BOLLA *takes the nail and she hammers it into a wooden support. She hangs her car keys on them.*

That's the nail the keys hang on. We'll keep them there, then any of us need to go somewhere we can just take them. If the keys are there, you can drive the car. When you've finished, they go back there. You don't have to ask.

BOLLA *starts to cry.*

I'm sorry. I should have . . . I've just damaged your wood.
I never asked. I'm sorry. I just . . . I just . . . I thought we
were going out.

Pause.

I'm sorry to both of you. I'm sorry. I'll make it up to you.

She cries.

I'm going to shut myself in there, and I'm not coming out
until I've done you a poem. And you can have it as a present
from me to you. And if it wins your competition, well then
I don't want none of the prize. It's yours. I'm going in there
now. I'll make it up to you Griffin. Goodnight. Goodnight
Jess.

Exit BOLLA. GRIFFIN *and* WATTMORE *stand there in
silence. The birds scream outside.*GRIFFIN *looks at the key,
hanging there on the hook. He puts his coat on. He picks
up his balaclava.*

WATTMORE. Where are you going? Griffin.

GRIFFIN. I . . . I set some traps out by the battery farm.
I forgot to check them.

WATTMORE. Don't go on the marsh. Griffin. Griffin. Don't
go on the Marsh. Don't go on the marsh.

WATTMORE *is left alone. Thunder. It starts to rain hard
on the tin roof.*

Blackout.

FIVE

Darkness. The storm is calmed. In the silence, the night heron passes low over the theatre, its scream-call ringing out, and fading over the black marsh.

The Cabin in the dead of night. Enter GRIFFIN, *in his balaclava, in the moonlight. He is out of breath. He takes the balaclava off. His nose is bloody. He goes to the stove to get warm. The firelight flares up in the room, revealing a rabbit hanging from the central beam. He stares at it hanging there. He unhooks it. He switches on the light. A lithe figure, with shoulder-length blonde hair is lying there, wrapped in a white sheet.*

GRIFFIN (*hissing*). Wattmore. WATTMORE!

WATTMORE *sits up.*

WATTMORE. What?

GRIFFIN. Get up.

WATTMORE. Griffin –

GRIFFIN. Get up.

WATTMORE. What's wrong? I'm on the cushions.

GRIFFIN. *Get up.*

WATTMORE *stands up, laboriously.*

WATTMORE. What time is it? Where have you been?

They both look at the BOY, *sleeping there.*

Who's that?

Silence.

GRIFFIN. Who's that? What?

WATTMORE. What?

GRIFFIN. What? I don't know. Who is it? Why did you let him in?

WATTMORE. I didn't let him in.

GRIFFIN. Well what's he doing here.

WATTMORE. How should I know?

Beat.

Is it a boy?

GRIFFIN. Okay.

Pause.

Wake him up.

WATTMORE. You wake him up. I'm not waking him up.

GRIFFIN. Wake him up Wattmore.

WATTMORE. Fuck off. I'm not waking him up.

GRIFFIN. What's he doing here? Wake him up.

WATTMORE. No.

GRIFFIN. Wake him up.

WATTMORE. No.

GRIFFIN. Wattmore.

WATTMORE. What?

Pause.

GRIFFIN. Stand back.

WATTMORE *does.*

WATTMORE. Griffin . . .

GRIFFIN. What?

WATTMORE. Put the rabbit down.

GRIFFIN *passes it to* WATTMORE. *He shakes the stranger once. He shakes him again.*

GRIFFIN. You.

Pause.

Boy.

WATTMORE. It might be a girl.

GRIFFIN. Shut up will you?

Beat.

You. Boy.

Beat.

Miss.

He shakes him again. He shakes him again. Harder. Very hard.

WATTMORE. Oh no.

GRIFFIN. What?

WATTMORE. Oh no. Is he . . . don't say . . . Oh Jesus. Is he cold?

GRIFFIN. Course he's cold. He's fucking starkers.

WATTMORE. Is he breathing?

GRIFFIN *listens.*

GRIFFIN. He's breathing.

Beat.

Okay Jess. What's going on?

WATTMORE. Nothing.

GRIFFIN. How did he get here.

WATTMORE. I don't know. What are you saying?

GRIFFIN. I come home there's a boy asleep on our couch.

WATTMORE. What are you saying? Where have you been Griffin. What happened to your face?

GRIFFIN. I went out. I fell over.

WATTMORE. What have you done Griffin?

GRIFFIN. I fell over.

WATTMORE. What's going on Griffin? Who is he?

GRIFFIN. Where's Bolla?

WATTMORE. She's in there. She's been in there all night.

GRIFFIN. Wake her up.

WATTMORE. No chance.

GRIFFIN. Wattmore . . .

WATTMORE. I'm not going in there.

GRIFFIN. I woke him up.

WATTMORE. No you didn't.

GRIFFIN. This is your fault.

WATTMORE. What. Why?

GRIFFIN. You were here. You were minding the fort.

WATTMORE. I was asleep.

They glare at one another in the moonlight.

GRIFFIN. Stand back.

He walks to the back door. He knocks on it.

GRIFFIN. Bolla.

He knocks harder. He goes in. Silence.

WATTMORE. The keys have gone. Griffin. And the tape recorder's gone. She's taken Dougal's recorder.

Re-enter GRIFFIN.

GRIFFIN. Is the car out there?

WATTMORE. She's gone out the window.

GRIFFIN. Wait here.

GRIFFIN *leaves through the strip plastic.* WATTMORE *approaches the youth. He reaches out a hand, but stops. He gasps.*

WATTMORE. Our father, who art in heaven, hallowed be thy name.

Re-enter GRIFFIN.

GRIFFIN. You can stop whispering now Jess. We're the only fuckers here. Who caught that rabbit? Jess. I didn't catch it. I've never went . . . I never went in the reeds. Who caught the rabbit? Jess? What are you doing. What's the matter? Jess?

Silence.

WATTMORE. It's an angel.

GRIFFIN (*simultaneous*). Angel.

Pause.

They both study him for a moment.

It's not.

Pause.

WATTMORE. How do you know? It could be.

GRIFFIN. It's not.

WATTMORE. It could be. Do you believe in angels?

WATTMORE *laughs quietly in wonder.*

Oh dear. Oh dear.

Pause.

I'm shivering. My hair's gone up my neck. (*He laughs.*) I prayed Griffin. Tonight. In here. I prayed for an angel. Look at his face. Do you . . . do you renounce Satan and his riddles and crimes?

GRIFFIN. Yes.

WATTMORE. Do you . . . do you . . . do you . . . I can't remember it. Do you renounce the fatted jackal? Do you renounce –

GRIFFIN. Yes.

WATTMORE. Do you spit his name?

GRIFFIN. I spit his name.

WATTMORE. I'm shivering. Will you kneel with me?

GRIFFIN. Yes.

WATTMORE. Will you begin.

GRIFFIN. Yes.

WATTMORE. Thank you Griffin. Grace to you. Grace to you.

They kneel in front of the iconostasis.

Do something easy.

Beat.

GRIFFIN. Behold . . . behold, I send an Angel before thee, to bring thee into the place which I have prepared . . . Beware –

WATTMORE. Beware of him, and obey his voice, provoke him not; for my name is in him. If thou shalt obey his voice, and do all that I speak; We're saved Griffin.

GRIFFIN. . . . then I will be an enemy unto thine enemies.

BOTH. For mine Angel shall go before thee . . . and I will cut them off.

WATTMORE. And ye shall serve the LORD your God, and he shall bless thy bread, and thy water; and I will take sickness away from the midst of thee.

Enter BOLLA. *She's soaked. She's holding the stereo in one hand and a dead rabbit by the feet in the other.*

GRIFFIN. Bolla.

WATTMORE. Bolla.

BOLLA. It's lashing it down.

GRIFFIN. Where have you been.

BOLLA. Catching rabbits.

GRIFFIN. What?

BOLLA. They're all over the road. Hundreds of 'em.

GRIFFIN. Wha –

BOLLA. My heart's pounding. Feel.

GRIFFIN. Bolla –

BOLLA. I got another in the car. There's hundreds out there.

GRIFFIN. Bolla. What's going on. Who is this?

BOLLA. Is he still asleep.

GRIFFIN. Do you know him?

BOLLA. I don't know him from Adam.

GRIFFIN. How did he get here?

BOLLA. I brung him.

GRIFFIN. Where from?

BOLLA. Cambridge.

GRIFFIN. Cambridge?

BOLLA. Yeah. He's a student.

GRIFFIN. A student of what?

BOLLA. I don't know. But I was hoping, of poetry.

GRIFFIN. What?

BOLLA. Yeah. But it's a bit fingers crossed. I know he knows about it.

GRIFFIN. How?

BOLLA. Because he was at a poetry night. In Corpus Christi.

GRIFFIN. You went to Cambridge tonight?

BOLLA. It's horrible. I spent an hour in the one-way system, it's like the fucking minotaur's maze. Bet it's easier getting in to study Greek than it is to drive your car in.

GRIFFIN. How did you find him?

BOLLA. On a noticeboard. They've got the lot, plays, black-tie piss ups, Karate, Late night this, all night that. These cunts'll do anything not to go to bed. So I went along, and sat at the back and I'm listening to them get up one after the other. And this one read out the first one I understood. And also, he looked quite small, so I followed him in the gents. And we chatted a bit. Then I asked him about what Corpus Christi meant, and before he could answer I gave him a left-hander then I stuffed him in the Golf.

WATTMORE. Oh no. Oh no.

BOLLA. I borrowed your recorder Jess. I hope you don't mind.

GRIFFIN. Why won't he wake up.

BOLLA. Right. He's had a lot of pills.

GRIFFIN. What?

BOLLA. He's had a lot of temazipan. Don't worry. He ain't going nowhere.

GRIFFIN. How many did you give him?

BOLLA. Not many.

GRIFFIN. How many?

BOLLA. Don't know really. Couple of handfuls.

GRIFFIN. Bolla. You could have killed him.

BOLLA. Come off it Griffin. He's a student. Have you seen what they get up to? You need the heart of a fucking bull. Look at him. He's having the time of his life.

GRIFFIN. Where's his clothes?

BOLLA. Right. Shortly after I got the pills down him, he had accident.

GRIFFIN. An accident.

BOLLA. Yes. He shat himself. At some point in the journey back, he shat himself in the boot of the car. Yeah. But don't worry. I burned 'em by the side of the road.

GRIFFIN. You burned his clothes.

BOLLA. I had to Griffin. They were festooned in shit. I thought you'd be pleased. I thought you were serious about this. I thought you wanted a poem.

GRIFFIN. I did.

BOLLA. Well there then. I thought it best to bring in an expert.

He stirs.

Here we go. Okay. First. We need some strong coffee. Get a
pint or two of that down him. Then we ask him about
poetry. Get him to do some, maybe get him to read yours.

GRIFFIN. But we'll go to prison.

BOLLA. Who's going to prison? Who's going to prison
Griffin. You think I'm a mug?

GRIFFIN. No.

BOLLA. You think I haven't planned this. One: he doesn't
know us. Two: he's got no idea where he is. Three: we're in
the middle of a fucking bog. And if he's not too much
trouble to us we'll have him back in a day or two. He'll
wake up naked on some lawn think it's all a hoot. Are you
in or out? Are you in or out Griffin?

The BOY *stirs.*

GRIFFIN. What do we do?

BOLLA. Switch off the light. Don't let him see us.

GRIFFIN *puts on his balaclava.*

What are you doing?

GRIFFIN. He'll see us.

BOLLA. You'll scare the shit out of him. Take it off.

GRIFFIN. He'll see me.

BOLLA. Griffin. You can't quiz him dressed like that. He won't
understand.

GRIFFIN. He's going to have a job understanding as it is.
Okay. We blindfold him.

BOLLA. How's he going to read if you blindfold him?

GRIFFIN. We read it to him. I'll read it aloud.

BOLLA. Griffin.

GRIFFIN. What?

BOLLA. Take the fucking balaclava off. Take it off.

GRIFFIN. Okay. Turn the light down.

> GRIFFIN *turns all of the lights off. Pitch dark. Silence.*

> I can't see a fucking thing. Wait.

> *He lights one lantern. The* BOY *sits up. The* BOY *stands up, naked in the half-light. He looks around him. From the shadows, the three of them advance, They stand ten feet away.* GRIFFIN *speaks very clearly.*

GRIFFIN. Who's your favorite poet?

BOLLA. Who in the field of poetry do you admire and why?

WATTMORE. Forgive me Jesus.

GRIFFIN. You. Who's . . . Who's your favorite poet? Say some poetry. Say some poetry.

BOLLA. Show him your poem.

GRIFFIN. Wait there.

> *He hands the poem to the* BOY.

> Read this. It's not finished. It's a first draft.

> *The* BOY *reads it.*

> Jess, get the boy a drink.

> WATTMORE *doesn't move. He stays seated, staring ahead.*

> He's thirsty Wattmore. Get the boy a drink. Get the boy a drink.

WATTMORE. I won't be part of this.

GRIFFIN. Wattmore.

> WATTMORE *does.*

> *The* BOY *looks at the page in his hand.*

> Well? What do you think?

WATTMORE. Here.

He hands him the water.

GRIFFIN. Out the way Wattmore.

Silence. The BOY *stands there.*

What do you think? Say something you little bastard. Would
it win? Would it win a prize. In your opinion. Could it win?

BOY. Cor . . .

BOLLA. Yes?

BOY. Cor . . .

GRIFFIN. Yes?

BOY. Corpus Christi. Corpus Christi means the body of Christ.

He passes out.

GRIFFIN. What the fuck? What the fuck was that?

BOLLA. I'll get him another miniature from the car. Hang
about.

GRIFFIN. Bolla –

BOLLA. Wait there. He needs a pick-me-up.

She runs out. GRIFFIN *runs into the back room to fetch
a blanket. Wattmore searches the cupboard for brandy.
He stops, and rises with a pair of brand new binoculars.*

GRIFFIN *runs back in with the blanket. He sees* WATTMORE
standing there holding the binoculars.

GRIFFIN. OK. Here's what we do. We –

He stops. They stand there in the silent room.

I found them. I found them in the reed beds.

Silence.

They're worth fifteen hundred pound Wattmore. I looked
them up on the internet. In the library. You can see in the
dark with them. And I found a buyer on the internet. In

Cambridge. They're going to pay six hundred pound for them. He's got the money today. I'm cycling in, and he's going to pay me.

Silence.

We've got nothing Wattmore. Rabbits. We've got rabbits. And if the town finds out. And the town comes here.

WATTMORE. Jack O'Lanterns. Jack O'Lanterns.

He drops the binoculars on the floor.

GRIFFIN. What are you doing? You clot.

Griffin picks them up.

Brilliant. You've shattered the lenses. I can't see anything now. It's pitch dark.

Re-enter BOLLA.

BOLLA. Don't panic but someone's coming up the road. They got torches. There's lots of them.

GRIFFIN. Oh Jesus.

BOLLA. Who are they?

GRIFFIN. It's no one.

BOLLA. We've got to get him out of here. Quick. Give me a hand with this one.

GRIFFIN. Put him in the back. Can we use your room.

BOLLA. Just give me a hand.

They carry the BOY *into the back room.*

WATTMORE. Are you there Prince? Are you there? Please. Are you there?

BOLLA *and* GRIFFIN *reappear.*

BOLLA. Who is it?

GRIFFIN. It's gypsies. Wattmore has had a disagreement with the gypsies.

BOLLA. Well we'll see them off.

WATTMORE. It's not gypsies.

BOLLA. What?

WATTMORE. They're coming to gather me. They want me in the ground.

Silence.

Bolla, you should go now.

BOLLA. I want to help Jess. Griffin? If there's any trouble I'm staying here. I'll look after you.

WATTMORE (*shouts*). You don't belong here. This isn't your home. You've done enough. Now leave.

Silence. She seems stunned. She looks at Jess for a long time.

BOLLA. I'm going to my room now. I'm going to look after the boy.

Exit BOLLA, into her room.

GRIFFIN. I just wanted to help. It's not too late Jess.

Noise outside. Breaking glass.

Get down. Switch off the light.

WATTMORE. I won't hide.

GRIFFIN switches off the light. Enter a MAN with a torch. GRIFFIN switches on the light. It is . . .

GRIFFIN. Royce.

ROYCE. Griffin. Jess. I'm not to speak to you. Where is she?

GRIFFIN. What do you want? It's the middle . . . it's five thirty in the morning.

ROYCE. I've brought one with me. We'll get to the bottom here.

Enter DOUGAL, with TWO WOMEN and a MAN. They all have torches. DOUGAL wears a black cloak.

DOUGAL. Where is she?

WATTMORE. Dougal.

DOUGAL. Jess Wattmore. Where is this witch?

ROYCE. She's in there.

DOUGAL. What has happened in this house. You keep a
woman here?

WATTMORE. She's a guest. She's paying rent.

DOUGAL. And she threatens my flock. She threatens a good
soul here. She would kill his babies. What is happening here
Jess Wattmore. And Floyd Fowler came and he spoke to me.
He spoke to me yesterday. He was after money. He's telling
lies Jess Wattmore. Tell me he is telling lies.

WATTMORE. He's telling lies.

DOUGAL. It's a black thing he's saying. It's a black, black
thing. An abomination. And I know from where it comes.
This woman. These tales. Griffin Montgomery. This is all
down to you now, is it not.

Silence.

GRIFFIN. Hello Dougal.

DOUGAL. Admit that it's down to you. Admit that you have
brought evil into this house. It's you who's to blame.

GRIFFIN. Yes. Yes. it is.

ROYCE. Hallelujah.

DOUGAL. And you're leading my man to the beast here.

GRIFFIN. Yes I am. I am leading him to the beast.

ROYCE. Hallelujah Jesus be praised . . .

DOUGAL. And you brazen out and say it. It's hell you worship.
Satan has you on a leash.

GRIFFIN. He does. It's hell I worship.

DOUGAL. There then. And they'll be a leaflet. And I'll
highlight your name in bold. Griffin Montgomery runs with
Jackals. There it is.

Silence.

GRIFFIN. Dougal. Do you remember when we were at school. Do you remember that day you shat in your own desk. Do you remember when you failed your Watermanship swimming, and you cried, and we laughed at you for crying, and do you remember you smeared shit all over the swimming pool changing rooms. And your mother, when she came in the middle of country dancing and mutilated her womanly parts with a fishknife. I'm just wondering if you remember any of what I'm remembering.

DOUGAL. It's a black mind you have. And you always did have.

GRIFFIN. There are so many things to say to you, but I'm going to just say this. You fucking leafblower. Leave this man be. He's not special. He's a gardener. He belongs in a garden.

ROYCE. I think you've said enough Griffin. It's Jess we should hear from now. He has a charge to answer.

WATTMORE. I'll answer it.

GRIFFIN. You don't have to say anything Jess Wattmore.

WATTMORE. Griffin.

GRIFFIN. This is no court of law and this is no copper.

WATTMORE. No. I want to tell them.

ROYCE. Do you mind if I take some notes? I suppose we should start at the beginning. Where were you on the day in question . . . ? The day Floyd Fowler brought his boy to Corpus Christi.

GRIFFIN. I was in the garden. I was working on the quince tree. I'd been working on it all day. I was in its branches, with a hand-saw, trying to stem the disease, you see. I had an idea that it was the left side which was sick, and that the right side could be saved, and it might grow back and in fifty, hundred years no-one would know the difference. Anyway, I was up in the Quince Tree, when the boy walks underneath.

ROYCE. Little Peter. Little Peter Fowler.

WATTMORE. Floyd's boy. Yes.

ROYCE. Did he speak to you? Did he say anything?

WATTMORE. He asks me where his dad is. And I said he could
    be in the Scholars Garden, he could be in the Chapel Garden,
    something like that. He could be anywhere see. So I said
    I don't know. I don't know where your dad is. Then the boy
    says he's cold, so I climbed down.

ROYCE. You climbed down.

WATTMORE. Yes. Well I could see he was shivering. His teeth
    were chattering.

ROYCE. So you climbed down the Quince Tree. Then what
    did you do.

WATTMORE. I took him into the potting shed.

GRIFFIN. That's enough now Wattmore.

WATTMORE. No Griffin. Let me tell it. I took him in the
    potting shed. I remember what time it was because I heard
    the bells of King's Chapel ring five times. And it was going
    dark, so I lit the lamp. I lit the lamp, and I turned the heater
    so the boy could get warm. It was dark now, I lit the lamp,
    and rubbed the boys hands to warm them up.

DOUGAL. And then what?

WATTMORE. And that was it. When he was warm, I buttoned
    up his coat, and he left me alone.

Pause.

I'm a good man.

DOUGAL. Do you swear Jess Wattmore. Do you swear this is
    what happened. The town will need the truth Jess. The town
    must know. Do you swear?

WATTMORE. On my eternal soul, and Jesus' eyes, and on the
    cross, I swear.

The BOY *appears from the back room, standing naked.*
Long pause.

BOY. Shelley.

ROYCE. What?

Pause.

BOY. What is heaven?
A globe of dew,
Filling in the morning new,
Some eyed flower whose young leaves waken,
On an unimagined world,
Constellated suns, unshaken
Orbits measureless, are furled.
In that frail and fading sphere,
With ten million gathered there,
To tremble, gleam and disappear.

Shelley.

He goes back into the room. He goes back inside. Closes the
door. Silence.

DOUGAL. Explain this Jess Wattmore.

Silence.

WATTMORE. I can't.

Silence.

I'm the Jack O'Lanterns. I robbed the man out on the marsh.
Here.

He shows the binoculars.

I beat him and I blinded him. I went out and I robbed him
and his boy, and I beat him with a hammer.

ROYCE. Is this true?

GRIFFIN. It's a lie.

DOUGAL. And Floyd Fowler's Boy? Is that a falsehood too?

WATTMORE. I touched Floyd Fowler's boy. I touched him.
I'm a grabber. I'm a dirty grabber, me. I'm the Jack
O'Lanterns. I'm the Jack O'Lanterns. I'm the will o'wisp.

Silence.

DOUGAL. The town shall know. Jess Wattmore. The town
shall know.

ROYCE. God rain down pity on your soul. And on this boy's.

Enter NEDDY.

DOUGAL. Leave this place Neddy Beagle. Leave this place.

Exit ROYCE, *and* DOUGAL, *and the others. Silence.*

NEDDY. Griffin.

GRIFFIN *stands there in silence.*

NEDDY. Well. I see you've found a buyer Griffin.

GRIFFIN. What?

NEDDY. I say I see you've found a buyer, for your car.

GRIFFIN. What do you mean?

NEDDY. I've just passed her on the road to Fen Ditton. A
woman it was. Going fast, but I saw her all right. It's not a
bad car, that. I'm glad for you too. We'll see an end to this
now. Will you come now Griffin?

GRIFFIN. What?

Pause.

Yes. Yes I will.

Pause.

I'm going to Cambridge Jess.

Pause.

I'm coming with you Neddy Beagle. We'll settle this
balance today.

GRIFFIN *puts his coat on. He picks up his gardening
equipment. He stops and picks up his poem. He looks at it.*

I know who'll win it. Someone who doesn't need it. Some
professor. Some girl. Some girl on her computer.

He burns the poem in the stove. Exit GRIFFIN. WATTMORE
*is left alone. The peal of church bells is heard. Dawn touches
the marsh outside the window. The distant church bells are
pealing.* WATTMORE *presses play on the tape recorder.
He goes into* BOLLA'*s room.*

TAPE. Then there was a war in heaven. Michael and his angels
under his command fought the dragon and his angels. And
the dragon lost the battle and was forced out of heaven.

He comes back out carrying the BOY *in his arms. He lays
him on the Chesterfield. He looks at him sleeping.*

This dragon – the ancient serpent called the Satan, the one
deceiving the whole world – was thrown down to earth with
all his angels.

*He bends over him, and kisses his cheek. He goes to the tall-
boy drawer and fetches his rope. The tape continues, as he
carries the rope into the back room, and closes the door.*

Then I heard a loud voice shouting across the heavens, 'It
has happened at last – They have defeated the Accuser by
the blood of the Lamb. By the blood of the Lamb has he
been thrown down. And they were not afraid to die. They
were not afraid to die.

WATTMORE'*s tin whistle is heard, playing alone on the
tape. Suddenly* BOLLA'*s voice jump cuts in on the tape.*

BOLLA'S VOICE. . . . to explain why I came here in the first
place. Anyway, I leave you my poem. I never wrote it down
because as you probably guessed I'm not much of a writer.
Or a reader. So I've spoke it instead, and perhaps if you
think it could win, one of you could jot it down. I always
liked you. It's called 'A Broken Bowl'.

Everything I touch ends up broken.
The dolls I had never had any heads.
When Good Bolla wakes up, the sun is shining,
She doth look out the window and behold the golden sun.
But when Bad Bolla wakes up,

She doth see a black sun in a black sky,
She doth see bad angels, pulling down the stars,
Burning the oxygen, she doth feel everything smashing down
Lying on its side
Like a broken bowl,
With the pieces still rocking.

We feel the moment when WATTMORE *hangs himself. The old wooden beams of the cabin bend and groan. Dust rains down from the beams in the sunlight. The birds cry out.*

The BOY *wakes up. He sits up, rubbing his eyes in the sunlight. He sits there rubbing his eyes. On the tape,* WATTMORE*'s tin-whistle resumes on the tape recorder. It stops, and the only sound is the birds out on the marsh.*

Enter a MAN *and a* BOY, *with a knapsack and binoculars, wrapped up against the cold.*

MAN. I don't mean to disturb you but the porch was open. Excuse me. Do you have a glass of water?

BOY. What? Yes.

MAN. Thank you. I see you have a view of the marsh. I am Tors. And you are?

BOY. Jonathan.

MAN. We are here on vacation. For two days. You know the night heron? We came to see him, but I think he has gone now. Do you know why he came?

JONATHAN. No.

MAN. How to explain . . . aahh. I don't know the word. I can't explain . . . Aaahh. In short, he was lost. He will have fought to stay on course, but the winds are too strong. It is the winds, you know. The winds decide in advance. But I think we were blessed that he was once among us, no? Have you seen him?

JONATHAN. No. I don't think . . . I don't think I have. Have you?

MAN. Nycticorax nycticorax. The native Indians called him The Night Angel. No. We have not seen him, no. But one day, perhaps. Maybe one day we shall see him.

They stand watching the light change across the broad marsh.

A Nick Hern Book

The Night Heron first published in Great Britain in 2002 as a
paperback original by Nick Hern Books Limited, 14 Larden Road,
London W3 7ST, in association with the Royal Court Theatre, London

Front cover: 'Folklore, Myths and Legends of Britain'
copyright © 1973, The Reader's Digest Association Ltd

Typeset by Country Setting, Kingsdown, Kent CT14 8ES
Printed and bound in Great Britain by Bookmarque, Croydon, Surrey

ISBN 1 85459 699 3

A CIP catalogue record for this book is available from
the British Library

ROYAL COURT

Royal Court Theatre presents

THE NIGHT HERON

by **Jez Butterworth**

First performance at the Royal Court Jerwood Theatre Downstairs
Sloane Square, London on 11 April 2002.

Supported by The Peter he Royal Court Theatre.